THE AESTHETIC OF

WALTER PATER

THE AESTHETIC OF

WALTER PATER

by Ruth C. Child

A WELLESLEY COLLEGE PUBLICATION

1969

OCTAGON BOOKS

New York

Reprinted 1969
by special arrangement with Wellesley College

OCTAGON BOOKS
A Division of Farrar, Straus & Giroux, Inc.
19 Union Square West
New York, N. Y. 10003

Library of Congress Catalog Card Number: 76-96153

Printed in U.S.A. by
TAYLOR PUBLISHING COMPANY
DALLAS, TEXAS

Foreword

THIS STUDY in its original form was written under the direction of Professor Clarence D. Thorpe, of the Department of English at the University of Michigan, and submitted to the Faculty of the University of Michigan in partial fulfilment of the requirements for the degree of Doctor of Philosophy. Since that time, the point of view of the writer has changed considerably, as further study of the material has brought further enlightenment. The work has therefore been completely rewritten, decreasing in length as it has grown and changed in substance. The author makes grateful acknowledgment to Professor Thorpe for his untiring aid, and for the stimulus of his keen mind which moves with such pleasure and power in the realm of critical theory. Thanks are due also to Professor Norman E. Nelson of the University of Michigan for generous assistance; to Professor Helen E. Patch of Mount Holyoke College for expert advice on the French material; to Professor Howard Mumford Jones, now of Harvard University, for incitement to further search for truth; and to Professor Anne K. Tuell of Wellesley College, whose enlightening criticism sent the book through the final stage in its growth.

Acknowledgments

Special thanks are due to the Macmillan Company for permission to quote extensively from the Library Edition of the *Works of Walter Pater,* and to use excerpts from *Walter Pater,* by Arthur Benson.

Acknowledgment is also made to the following publishers for permission to print copyright material:

To George Allen and Unwin, Ltd., for selections from *Modern Painters,* by John Ruskin.

To Calmann-Lévy, Éditeurs, for selections from *La vie littéraire,* by Anatole France.

To William Heinemann, Ltd., for selections from *The Complete Works of Swinburne,* edited by E. Gosse and T. J. Wise.

To Houghton Mifflin Company for selections from *The Drift of Romanticism,* by Paul Elmer More.

To the Liveright Publishing Corporation for selections from *Sketches and Reviews,* by Walter Pater.

To John W. Luce and Company for selections from *The Works of Oscar Wilde,* edited by R. Ross.

To the Modern Language Association for permission to use in a different form material previously printed in an article entitled "Is Walter Pater an Impressionistic Critic?" *Publications of the Modern Language Association,* December, 1938.

To Kegan Paul, Trench, Trübner, and Company, Ltd., for selections from *The Introduction to Hegel's Philosophy of Fine Art,* translated by Bernard Bosanquet.

To Charles Scribner's Sons for selections from *The Sense of Beauty,* by George Santayana.

Table of Contents

THE AESTHETIC OF WALTER PATER

Introduction

B EING SO CLOSE to the modern day but not of it, Walter
Pater is denied the appreciation bestowed on many a
minor author of days further past. Though actually so recent,
his work comes to us almost from another world. Even while it
portrays movingly the bewildering flux of things, it carries an
atmosphere of the incredibly stable. It has no hints of war's
alarms, no shrinking from the conflicts of the masses, no perception of social need. The problem which occupies Pater is not
our difficulty of holding together the very framework of society,
but the permanent human problem of the transitory nature of
all things and the irremediable pain of the world.

In another way Pater is not of our time. He won fame as a
great stylist. But now, as our sentences grow shorter and shorter,
and our units of thought break up, we forget our artistic herit-
age, and scorn him as artificial, over-elaborate, 'precious.'
Likewise as a critic Pater is denied his just dues, and dismissed
as 'impressionistic' or 'aesthetic.' The first term embodies a
misunderstanding, which springs from reading a very small
part of his work as typical of the whole. The second term rests
also partly on a misunderstanding, but is more largely a reflection of his philosophy of life and of art. In these strenuous
days we moderns feel that anyone who talks about beauty and
neglects to discuss the social significance of art is shallow, not
to be taken seriously.

1

The Aesthetic of Walter Pater

All these differences, real though they are, do not lessen Pater's true stature. They may dwarf him in our eyes. But when this epoch of world change is past—as epochs do pass—Pater will still be found dealing graciously with the central human problem, how to live. In style, too, his place is sure. The desire for intricately wrought perfection, for subtlety in matter and manner, is a permanent instinct in the artist. Lyly, Sir Thomas Browne, Pater, and their kind are surely of close kin to the artists of tomorrow, when the recurring beat of complexity shall alternate again with the beat of simplicity. And in criticism, too, Pater will have much to give the future. His work will be read as a whole; and his neglect of social issues will no longer obscure the fine intelligence, the concern for human values, of his critical work.

The dismissal of Pater as "aesthetic"—in style, in critical viewpoint, in philosophy of life—is largely a matter of the last thirty years. In his own day, criticism of his writing was predominantly enthusiastic, with praise of his beautiful style, his sound learning, his knowledge of the ancient world. Saintsbury was one of his admirers,[1] and Bosanquet looked up to him as a great scholar and critic, citing him as authority on the history of the Renaissance.[2]

To be sure, popular gossip would appear to have been less favorable than the criticism of the periodicals, largely because of the extravagance of the group led by Wilde who claimed to be his disciples. But Pater held himself off from his "followers," and set forth his true philosophy in *Marius the Epicurean,* which was received with great praise. The general trend

---

[1] See especially *Modern Criticism* (New York, 1904), III, 546.
[2] *History of Aesthetic* (2nd ed., London, 1904), pp. xiii, 239, 251.

Introduction

of written criticism during his lifetime was distinctly favorable.[1]

The first two books about Pater, appearing nine and twelve years after his death, also dealt with him favorably, and fairly. Ferris Greenslet's little volume of 1903 [2] contained a penetrating though very brief discussion of his writings. And the excellent biography by Arthur C. Benson in 1906 [3] presented an engaging picture of a shy Oxford don who did his college work conscientiously, with real interest in his students, lived in simple but beautiful chambers, and put his whole soul into expressing in polished perfection his intelligent, sensitive reflections on art and life.

But a change in attitude began in 1907 when Thomas Wright wrote his two-volume biography,[4] and damned a good friend with his praise. From then on for many years, the main note in the studies of Pater has been emphasis on the "aesthetic" character of his work—that is, its remoteness from life, its over-refinement, its interest in the morbid and the curious, its lack of moral values. This note predominated through the obviously superficial study by Edward Thomas,[5] the attacks by the Humanists, particularly Paul Elmer More [6] and T. S. Eliot,[7] the metaphysical analyses by German schol-

[1] See reviews listed under "Renaissance" and "Marius the Epicurean" in bibliography.

[2] *Walter Pater,* Contemporary Men of Letters Series, New York.

[3] *Walter Pater,* English Men of Letters Series, London.

[4] *The Life of Walter Pater,* London.

[5] *Walter Pater, A Critical Study,* London, 1913.

[6] *Nation,* XCII (April 13, 1911), 365–80, reprinted in *Shelburne Essays,* Series VIII, New York, 1913.

[7] "Arnold and Pater," *Bookman,* LXXII (Sept. 1930), 1–7, reprinted in *Selected Essays,* London, 1933, and in *The Eighteen-Eighties,* ed. W. de la Mare, Cambridge, 1930.

3

The Aesthetic of Walter Pater

ars,[1] and even the brilliant study in 1931 by Miss Rosenblatt in her *L'idée de l'art pour l'art dans la littérature anglaise. pendant la période victorienne.*[2]

As a sample judgment we may take this from Paul Elmer More:

> Paterism might without great injustice be defined as the quintessential spirit of Oxford emptied of the wholesome intrusions of the world—its pride of isolation reduced to sterile self-absorption, its enchantment of beauty alembicated into a faint Epicureanism, its discipline of learning changed into a voluptuous economy of sensations, its golden calm stagnated into languid elegance.[3]

Along with the stress in all these studies on Pater's aestheticism went the stress on the so-called impressionistic character of his criticism. The Humanists have been particularly bitter against him as an impressionist, by which they mean a person who substitutes for a sound interpretation or judgment of a work of art his own purely personal impressions. This view of his criticism is predominant in practically all the works from Thomas Wright to the present. It has combined with the stress on his aestheticism to give us the picture of a critic who stands apart from the main stream of English critical thought, and indulges his own charming fancies without any solid foundation of critical judgment. The praise given by Oliver Elton, who called him "our greatest critic since Coleridge," [4] was distinctly out of line with the prevailing view.

[1] Staub, Friedrich, *Das imaginäre Porträt Walter Paters,* Un. of Zurich, 1926; Proesler, Hans, *Pater und sein Verhältnis zur deutschen Literatur,* Un. of Freiburg (Breisgau), 1917.

[2] Bibliothèque de la Revue de littérature comparée, LXX, Paris, 1931.

[3] *Shelburne Essays,* Series VIII, p. 108.

[4] *Survey of English Literature, 1830–1890* (London, 1920), I, 279.

Introduction

In the last few years, however, we have had signs that the tide is turning. In 1931 there appeared a distinguished study by A. J. Farmer of *Walter Pater as a Critic of English Literature*;[1] and in 1933 came an analysis by Miss Helen H. Young, *The Writings of Walter Pater, a Reflection of British Philosophical Opinion from 1860–1890*.[2] In these studies, full credit is given not only to Pater's emotional sensitivity, and to his cultivated sense of style, but to the substratum of thought which underlay his whole work. He begins to appear not merely as an aesthete and a stylist but as a thinker.

For our own sakes this better understanding should be encouraged. We cannot afford to dismiss with impatience so sensitive and discriminating a man of letters as Walter Pater because he is a step behind and a step ahead of the modern temper. Studies of many kinds could well be made—studies of his interpretations of Greek philosophy and art, his relation to the German romantic philosophers, his continuity with the English critics before him. The study of which we feel most need is a new biography, which shall throw some light on the forces which shaped his personality; we wish, above all things, to know why he saw the whole world in terms of beauty or its contrary, and why he concerned himself with seeing and feeling rather than with doing. The materials for such a biography are lacking at the present time; perhaps they are gone beyond our reach forever. But there are many other illuminating approaches which can be adopted. The task undertaken in this book is an analysis of Pater's aesthetic theory,

[1] *Walter Pater as a Critic of English Literature, a Study of "Appreciations,"* Grenoble.
[2] Bryn Mawr College.

with the aim of presenting the consistent framework on which it was built, and its gradual development within that framework. Such an analysis is bound to lead to a better understanding of his criticism, and of his whole personality. Such an analysis throws light also, by contrast and suggestion, on the many types of criticism preferred or practiced by other men.

As a brief preliminary to a detailed study of Pater's aesthetic, it is well to see him against the background of his time. He belonged, we say now, to the "aesthetic movement." He himself would probably have denied it, for he held himself aloof from any group, so successfully that a contemporary defense of *The Aesthetic Movement in England,* written in 1882 by Walter Hamilton, discusses Rossetti, Morris, Swinburne, O'Shaughnessy, and Wilde, but makes no mention of Pater. The perspective of time has brought enlightenment, however, and we can now see him in his historical place.

The nineteenth-century development of thought called the aesthetic movement is sometimes loosely dubbed "art for art's sake," since it was, in fact, a very rough approximation to the earlier French *l'art pour l'art.* It was, summarily speaking, a movement to restore art to its true place in the scheme of human values. The very heart of it was a love of beauty in all its forms, a conviction gained by keen experience that beauty is intensely pleasurable, deeply valuable. This came in an unbroken line from the romantic period, where Keats was perhaps its foremost exemplar—"Beauty is truth, truth beauty,—that is all Ye know on earth, and all ye need to know." In the early Victorian days, it was Ruskin who stood forth as the champion of beauty, both through his art criticism and his campaign to remake society so that the values of artistic creation could be enjoyed by all.

Against the influences which worked for art and beauty, the Victorian public seemed arrayed. It was, naturally, a bourgeois public, newly formed by the rise of the middle classes, with cheap tastes, a worship of material prosperity, and an inclination to insist that art should obviously instruct or uplift. A good deal of the best prose of the period was an attack on Victorian standards. Carlyle vociferated against the worship of Mammon, and Arnold preached sweet reason against the Philistines. Ruskin, too, attacked the blindness to beauty, the commercialism, and the smug reliance on material prosperity of his day.

But it was the aesthetic group which came forward especially in the service of art and beauty, sometimes from the angle of creation, sometimes in battle against the bourgeois, making the attack which is proverbially the best defense. Its members worked in many fields. Chief among them were the poet-painters Rossetti and Morris, the painters Burne-Jones and Whistler, the poet Swinburne, the critic Pater, the dramatist Wilde, all standing out against a background of lesser men. Their enthusiasm was given to all varieties of beautiful things, ranging from a statue or poem to a landscape in nature; and they wished to make life lovely by beautiful surroundings— furniture, art-objects, "blue china," perhaps even a more attractive style of dress. The most extreme point of the movement was reached with Wilde, and its influence has continued in different ways down to the present, with Arthur Symons as its most persistent literary exponent.

The movement had many facets, as these different temperaments reacted in different ways to the influences around them. In some of its aspects Pater had no part. For instance, his gracious spirit never turned to bitterness or rebellion. In England, as in France, the cheap tastes of the reading public, their overstrict standards of morality, and their inclination to insist that literature should be written to instruct or uplift aroused a deep antagonism on the part of some authors, and a tendency to produce literature which offended against the prevailing moral code. Swinburne and Wilde shared in both these manifestations of revolt, but Pater shared in neither. He was completely without bitterness on any score, and never attacked any group whatever. His own moral code was very high, and he took no issue with the prevailing standards of morality.

Another aspect of the aesthetic movement in which Pater had no share was its social or humanitarian side. This was peculiar to England and had no parallel in the French *l'art pour l'art*. Morris followed Ruskin in wishing to reorganize society so as to make the satisfactions and releases of art possible for all. Morris and Wilde were particularly interested in putting beauty into the utilitarian objects of everyday life. In these social concerns Pater had no part.

He did, however, share the aesthetic interest in the sensuous elements of art, evident in England as in France; evident, for instance, in Ruskin's practical art criticism, in the painting of Rossetti, Whistler, and Burne-Jones, the poems of Rossetti, Morris, and Swinburne, and the literary history of John Symonds. He had an unusually strong appreciation of sensuous beauty in art and nature, and a notable ability to convey vivid sense impressions in his own writing.

8

Introduction

Another feature of the movement on both sides of the channel was the intermingling of the arts. Here Pater was also at one with the group. The Pre-Raphaelite Brotherhood had attempted in their painting to imitate Keats' poetry; Rossetti and Morris were trying to put pictures in verse; while certain minor poets, like O'Shaughnessy, were writing "Poems in Marble." Pater's own interests were wide. He was not a literary critic only, but a critic of the arts, including painting, sculpture, architecture, and literature. He called himself, therefore, an "aesthetic" critic, or a critic of all things beautiful.

His exotic interests also reflect certain currents in the aesthetic movement: his interest, for instance, in Gautier, Flaubert, and Heine; his admiration for the elaborate and precious Latin of the Empire of the second century; and his romantic interpretation of certain aspects of Greek art and religion. On the other hand, his tremendous enthusiasm for Goethe gives him a point of view closer to that of Arnold than is ordinarily noticed.

Pater's writing had, likewise, the faintly melancholy tone characteristic of most of the aesthetic group both in England and France. But as that melancholy permeated much of European literature in the nineteenth century, we cannot consider it as binding him to the aesthetic group in particular.

The characteristics so far mentioned are non-controversial. It is readily granted that Pater shared the aesthetic interest in a variety of arts, in the sensuous elements of art, and in the exotic; and that he lacked both the rebellion and the social concern of certain members of the English group. There are, however, several points which need to be clarified and elabo-

9

rated, for an understanding both of his aesthetic theory, and of his place in the aesthetic movement. It is these points with which this book will primarily deal.

The first of these is Pater's attitude toward the theory of art for art's sake, which was held by certain members of the aesthetic group in England, as by all the followers of *l'art pour l'art* in France. Swinburne, in his younger days, was an exponent of the theory, and Wilde upheld it throughout his literary career. This study will show that Pater, like Swinburne, developed beyond the idea to a more mature point of view. He began his work with an emphasis on art for art's sake, but progressed gradually to a greater and greater emphasis on the ethical function of art, thus returning, as Swinburne had returned, to the essentials of the long English tradition. During this progress he held steadily to the idea that art is an expression of the individual personality. At first he laid much stress on the power of art to give the beholder sheer intensity, intellectual and emotional excitement. Later he came to believe that art actually enlarges and purifies the soul, by developing the emotions and intellect and by holding up a vision of the ideal.

Another element in the English aesthetic movement had Pater as one of its main supporters. He held undeviatingly that the creation of beauty demanded perfection of form, which could be attained only by the most patient, devoted effort. In his belief in the overwhelming importance of form in art, and his preoccupation with the relation between form and content, he was strikingly similar to the French group, much more like them than like any of his English contemporaries, even Wilde. He was like them, also, in his emphasis on the necessity of self-conscious, deliberate artistry, which, we shall see, he stressed more and more strongly as the years went by.

Pater also played a particularly important part in a phase of the English aesthetic movement not paralleled in the French *l'art pour l'art,* an insistence on the relation between art and life. Ruskin and Morris had wished to beautify the lives of the English people by remaking the social order, and by making artistic the utilitarian objects of daily life. Now Pater brought a new idea, his most original contribution to the movement, and an integral part of his aesthetic theory. He taught that each man could make his own life beautiful by treating it in the spirit of art, living it as an end in itself. This conception of life as an art was picked up by a group of younger disciples, particularly Wilde, and distorted into a caricature of itself, so that many people now think of the aesthetic movement as producing merely the "aesthete" and the "arty" poseur. It is important, therefore, to study Pater's own idea of the artistic life and see what it really did imply. As he developed in his understanding of the function of art, he progressed also in his attitude toward life, stressing more and more strongly the unity running through the diversity of the universe, and the need of living always in the self-created ideal.

Finally, Pater's own particular type of criticism must be studied. He had one consistent critical aim, to find and convey the 'formula,' the characteristic quality of each man's work. His intentions have often been misunderstood, and the words 'aesthetic' and 'impressionistic' applied to him in inaccurate fashion. A comprehension of his critical theory and practice

11

will clear away these misunderstandings; and a knowledge of his developing theories of art and life will enable us to appreciate the deepening tone of his criticism, a criticism so keen and discriminating, so rich and humane, as to rank him among the best of nineteenth-century critics.

CHAPTER I

The Function of Art

1. 'ART FOR ART'S SAKE' IN PATER'S EARLY WORK

A T THE TIME Walter Pater began writing, the term 'art for art's sake' was a derogatory catchword in England, calling to mind ivory towers, stinging kisses, and *Fleurs du Mal*. But to the real artists who used it, it had an earnest significance not at all understood by the masses. It was a declaration of the freedom of art from all alien demands. The artist was to reject with determination every competing claim. He was not to write in the interests of morality, religion, humanitarian progress, popular favor, commercial gain, or even the revelation of his own personality. He was to work only in the service of beauty, obedient to no laws save the laws of art, devoted to art for its own sake.

In Pater's early work this idea was dominant, set forth strikingly in the brilliant essays in the *Renaissance*. There Leonardo da Vinci appears as an artist who worked for no other end than the love of the beauty created:

> Other artists have been as careless of present or future applause, in self-forgetfulness, or because they set moral or political ends above the ends of art; but in him this solitary culture of beauty seems to have hung upon a kind of self-love, and a carelessness in the work of art of all but art itself. Out of the secret places of a unique temperament he brought strange blossoms and fruits hitherto unknown; and for him,

the novel impression conveyed, the exquisite effect woven, counted as an end in itself—a perfect end.[1]

Botticelli also is a creator who "sets for himself the limits within which art, undisturbed by any moral ambition, does its most sincere and surest work." [2] The essay on Winckelmann deals in terms of highest praise with a man who gave himself up to art alone.

Throughout the *Renaissance* Pater's emphasis on art for art's sake is accompanied by a frequent disparagement of moral values in favor of artistic perfection. The medieval *contefable Aucassin and Nicolette* he describes thus:

> Rough as it is, the piece certainly possesses this high quality
> of poetry, that it aims at a purely artistic effect. Its subject
> is a great sorrow, yet it claims to be a thing of joy and re-
> freshment, to be entertained not for its matter only, but
> chiefly for its manner, it is *cortois,* it tells us, *et bien assis.*[3]

Though Leonardo "handles sacred subjects continually, he is the most profane of painters," because "no one ever ruled over the mere *subject* in hand more entirely" than he, or "bent it more dextrously to purely artistic ends." [4] Winckelmann went over to the Roman Catholic Church in order that he might have patronage at court and be sent to Rome; but he is to be absolved for this painful loss of sincerity because he was sac-rificing a lesser part of his nature for a more important: in him "the moral instinct, like the religious or political, was merged in

---

[1] P. 117. All Pater references are to the Library Edition, London, Macmillan, 1910, except references to *Sketches and Reviews* (New York, Boni and Liveright, 1919), and *Uncollected Essays* (Portland, Maine, T. B. Mosher, 1903), which are not included in that edition.

[2] P. 55.   [3] P. 18.   [4] P. 119.

the artistic." [1] The Greek art which the great German scholar so loved is presented as more vital than the Greek religion, which had the "privilege" of being able "to transform itself into an artistic ideal." [2] Much of the essay, emphasizing Winckelmann's interest in the concrete and sensuous, his passionate friendships with beautiful youths, and his love of beautiful form, seems to make the values of sensuous beauty supreme.

The doctrine of art for art's sake which Pater espoused at the outset of his career had both a philosophical background and an immediate *raison d'être*. Its philosophical basis had been thoroughly worked out by the German romantic philosophers from Kant through Hegel, who were intent on distinguishing between the values of different types of human experience. And these theoretical considerations had come to practical expression in the revolt of certain conscientious artists, both in England and abroad, against an uncomprehending public. In France in the second quarter of the nineteenth century, the reformist minorities had tried to draw the writers into an arraignment of social injustice, while the bourgeois majority had depreciated art altogether, paying tribute only to gains in science and industry. The bourgeois public was superficial also in its moral standards, and considered many harmless or earnestly ethical works as outside the moral pale. It was no wonder that a group of younger writers followed Gautier in raising the standard of *l'art pour l'art*. The movement crystallized shortly after the Revolution of 1848. Gautier, Flaubert, Baudelaire, Leconte de Lisle, Banville, and the Goncourts were the first group of rebels, followed in the

[1] P. 187.   [2] P. 204.

sixties and seventies by some of the younger Parnassians, particularly Heredia.[1]

In England, too, it was the climate of the times which helped to turn certain serious artists toward art for art's sake.[2] As the middle classes became more and more the readers of literature in the nineteenth century, they wished it to conform to their own constricted standards of practical activity, strict morals, and narrow common sense. The Utilitarian philosophy was a reinforcement to this anti-aesthetic attitude. Both Ruskin and Morris labored earnestly to convince England that beauty was necessary to the full life, and both did much to educate bourgeois taste. But in spite of their efforts canons of taste were ill-founded. Run-of-the-mill critics, reviewing in the periodicals, too often judged a writer merely by whether his work tended to uphold the prevailing moral standard.[3] To the artist irked by this constant moral emphasis, even the great critics like Carlyle, Ruskin, and Arnold might seem at times to strike too forcibly the moral note. The painter, said Ruskin in one of his ministerial moments, has the same task as the preacher. "Both are commentators on infinity, and the duty of both is to take for each discourse one essential truth, . . . and to impress that, and that alone, upon those whom they address." [4]

Even a high-minded artist might shudder away from all this, and say to the world, "Not so, my moral friends. My art

[1] For an account of the origins of the movement, see Albert Cassagne, *La théorie de l'art pour l'art en France,* Paris, 1906.

[2] For an account of the origins of the idea in England, see Louise Rosenblatt, *L'idée de l'art pour l'art.*

[3] Rosenblatt, pp. 25–44.

[4] *Modern Painters,* I, pt. II, sec. 1, ch. 4, § 4, Complete Works (ed. E. T. Cook and A. Wedderburn, London, 1903–12), III, 157.

is not for the sake of religion, or of ethical perfection, or of material service. It is for the production of beauty. I serve art for art's sake alone." That was the reaction of Morris, who says in the Apology with which he begins the *Earthly Paradise,* "Why should I strive to set the crooked straight?"

Though the essential idea had a slow growth from its germinating point with the romantic critics,[1] it was Swinburne who first became known as an exponent of art for art's sake, importing the French dogmas and phrases. He associated himself with the group of *l'art pour l'art* by his essay in praise of Baudelaire, in 1862, and did valiant work for the next six years in attempting to free art from the shackles of morality. His *Notes on Poems and Reviews* is a virulent reply to the critics who had attacked his own work on moral grounds, and the long essay on Blake, published in 1868, devotes many pages to an exposition of the theory of art for art's sake and a diatribe against art's trying to serve science or religion or morality, or any other end.[2]

In the energy of their reaction against alien demands, both the French and English exponents of the theory put their point in exaggerated form. Gautier quoted Baudelaire approvingly:

Si le poète a poursuivi un but moral, il a diminué sa force poètique; et il n'est pas imprudent de parier que son oeuvre sera mauvaise. La poèsie ne peut pas, sous peine de mort ou de déchéance, s'assimiler à la science ou à la morale; elle n'a pas la Vérité pour objet, elle n'a qu'Elle-même.[3]

[1] Rosenblatt, chs. 2, 3.

[2] For Swinburne's part in the movement, see G. Lafourcade, *La Jeunesse de Swinburne* (Paris, London, 1928), II, *passim.*

[3] "Charles Baudelaire," *Portraits et souvenirs littéraires* (Paris, 1875), p. 186; quoted from Baudelaire's "Gautier" (1859), *L'art romantique,* Oeuvres complètes (ed. Gautier, Paris, 1923), IV, 97.

Swinburne expressed the idea in his own vigorous fashion, in his 1868 monograph on Blake.

> Art is not like fire or water, a good servant and a bad master; rather the reverse. She will help in nothing, of her own knowledge or freewill: upon terms of service you will get worse than nothing out of her. Handmaid of religion, exponent of duty, servant of fact, pioneer of morality, she cannot in any way become; she would be none of these things though you were to bray her in a mortar. . . . It is at her peril, if she tries to do good.[1]

With such ideas in the air about him, it is not surprising that the young Pater should show himself an enthusiast for 'art for art's sake.' Not only was he personally acquainted with Swinburne, but he also knew well a group including John Payne, Arthur O'Shaughnessy, and Simeon Solomon, all of whom professed to belong to the art for art's sake school.[2] Furthermore, he read a good deal of modern French literature, which was filled with references to the battle of *l'art pour l'art*. Particularly he must have come across the art for art's sake theory in the works of Gautier. It does not seem likely that Flaubert and Baudelaire played any considerable part in developing his critical theories. True, he was early familiar with the writings of Flaubert, and for a long period trained himself in the technique of expression by translating a page a day from the latter as well as from Sainte-Beuve.[3] But Flaubert's critical ideas did not come to publication till after his

[1] Complete Works (ed. E. Gosse and T. J. Wise, London, 1925–27), XVI, 137.
[2] Wright, I, 230–1.
[3] Wm. Sharp, "Personal Reminiscences of Walter Pater," *Atlantic*, LXXIV (Dec. 1894), 806.

18

The Function of Art

death, when his *Correspondance* was published in 1887 and 1889, at which time Pater read the two successive volumes with admiration, and wrote a review of each.[1] We have no evidence of his familiarity with Baudelaire till 1888.[2] But he was evidently acquainted with Gautier very early. The latter's influence is apparent in the essays on *Winckelmann*,[3] *Leonardo da Vinci*,[4] and *Wordsworth*,[5] and in the *Postscript* to *Appreciations*.[6]

Not only was Pater familiar with French and English expressions of the idea, however, but he was well acquainted also with its background in philosophic theory. His early reading in aesthetics included a thorough study at Oxford of Hegel's *Philosophy of Fine Art*,[7] Hegelianism having just been introduced to Oxford students by Thomas Hill Green. Hegel, among other German romantic philosophers, had given a careful development to the idea of art for art's sake.[8] Like Kant, Schiller, and Schelling, he had insisted that art has no aim outside itself, though by its own high nature it exalts the

---

[1] "The Life and Letters of Gustave Flaubert," and "Correspondance de Gustave Flaubert," *Sketches and Reviews*.

[2] A. Beyer, *Walter Paters Beziehungen zur Französischen Literatur und Kultur*, Studien zur Englischen Philologie, LXIII (1931), 70–1.

[3] B. Fehr, "Walter Paters Beschreibung der Mona Lisa und Théophile Gautiers romantischer Orientalismus," *Archiv für das Studium der Neueren Sprachen und Literaturen*, CXXXV (1916), 80–102; and J. S. Harrison, "Pater, Heine, and the Old Gods of Greece," *PMLA*, XXXIX (Sept. 1924), 655–6.

[4] *Ibid.*

[5] *Appre.*, p. 43.

[6] Pp. 243, 253.

[7] See Bernhard Fehr, "Walter Pater und Hegel," *Englische Studien* (1916), L, 2, pp. 300–8.

[8] See Rose Egan, "The Genesis of the Theory of 'Art for Art's Sake' in Germany and in England," Smith Studies in Modern Languages, II, no. 4, July 1921, and V, no. 3, April 1924.

nature of man. Denying any extrinsic end, such as moral improvement, he says:

> Against this it is necessary to maintain that art has the vocation of revealing *the truth* in the form of sensuous artistic shape . . . and, therefore, has its purpose in itself, in this representation and revelation. For other objects, such as instruction, purification, improvement, pecuniary gain, endeavor after fame and honor, have nothing to do with the work of art as such, and do not determine its conception.[1]

To the young Pater, Goethe was also a source of constant inspiration. And Goethe had reinforced the same idea. "To demand a moral aim of the artist," he had said, "is to ruin his work." [2]

The net effect of a man's doctrine, however, depends not only on its various ingredients, but also on their proportion. The idea of art for art's sake may be a segment of a well-balanced theory. It may, that is, be the insistence which the public occasionally needs that an artist is not a preacher or a social reformer, but a creator with his own aims and tools. And yet it may at the same time be combined with the other half of the truth—that even though art is pursued for its own sake, it does at the same time contribute to the ethical nature of man, enlarging the very stature of his soul.

The German romantic philosophers had always maintained this wise balance. Hegel, with whom Pater was most familiar,

[1] *Introduction to the Philosophy of Fine Art* (trs. B. Bosanquet, London, 2nd ed., 1905), pp. 141–2.
[2] *Dichtung und Wahrheit*, Sämtliche Werke (Jubiläums-Ausgabe, 1902–7), XXIV, T. III, B. 12, S. 112.

had laid much stress on art as the expression of the Truth, the sensuous embodiment of the Absolute Idea. He taught that the aesthetic experience provides us with a sort of sample of truth, in that it gives us a harmonious experience in which the good has been achieved out of conflict.[1] Pater's other German master, Goethe, spoke in less metaphysical terms, but his point of view was also well balanced. To him art was inevitably the expression of personality. What the artist must do, therefore, is by no means to attempt to improve or instruct mankind, but simply to make of himself a better, richer person. "If a poet has as high a soul as Sophocles, his influence will always be moral, let him do what he will." [2]

On the other hand, the French writers of *l'art pour l'art* had been guilty of a serious lack of proportion. They held, to be sure, that God is the foundation of beauty, the perfectly beautiful, and almost all of them spoke interchangeably of Beauty, the Ideal, and the Divine.[3] They agreed with Baudelaire that "la beauté est une qualité si forte qu'elle ne peut qu'ennoblir les âmes." [4] But though they felt that beauty was from God, and exalted the soul, they did not say so often enough or insistently enough to make an impression. They were too busy fighting for their right to create as they pleased to place a proportionate emphasis on the ethical role of art.

[1] *Philosophy of Fine Art* (trs. F. P. B. Osmaston, London, 1920), I, 125–44 (intro. to Pt. I).

[2] J. P. Eckermann, *Gespräche mit Goethe* (Leipzig, 1876), Part III (Mar. 28, 1827), p. 90.

[3] The Goncourts were an exception. Leconte de Lisle, in spite of his opposition to Christianity, believed in a divine spirit, and considered beauty the manifestation of it.

[4] "Barbier" (1861), *L'art romantique*, Oeuvres, IV, 26. Baudelaire derived many of his ideas from Poe's writings, especially from the *Poetic Principle*, 1850.

The Aesthetic of Walter Pater

Swinburne, in his younger days, had shown the same lack of proportion as his French models. While he believed that true art would inevitably be moral, his battle against the "heresy of instruction" carried him to extremes. His literary practice also obscured the ethical elements of art production, for he wrote of a passionate, fleshly love which contemporaries called lust. His period of youthful rebellion lasted until 1867, when he began to write poems in furtherance of Mazzini's struggles for the freedom of Italy, and was progressively drawn away from the tendencies of *l'art pour l'art*.

The young Pater's point of view also lacked balance. Though he had behind him English romantic criticism with its strong emphasis on the power of art to quicken and enlarge, and though the German criticism which he so much admired had a pronounced ethical strain, his own early work was, on its shimmering surface, careless of ethical values. To his later dismay, his celebration of artistic perfection as an end in itself produced a group of disciples who, in striving for beauty for its own sake, forgot that true beauty includes spiritual as well as sensuous loveliness.

To be sure, even in his first book he recognized the value of art as an aid to the best life. The Conclusion tells us that what man most desires is "a quickened sense of life," "a quickened, multiplied consciousness."

> Of such wisdom the poetic passion, the desire of beauty, the love of art for its own sake, has most. For art comes to you proposing frankly to give nothing but the highest quality to your moments as they pass, and simply for those moments' sake.[1]

[1] P. 239.

22

The Function of Art

There is no contradiction here, though Pater speaks in the same breath of art for the sake of art, and art for the sake of life. Appreciation of beauty is to be the direct aim, enhancement of life the indirect result.

But though the Conclusion does not fail to recognize life as higher than art, it has nevertheless a somewhat dubious ring, because the values which it asks of life are hardly the highest. It presents as the greatest good sheer intensity, intellectual and emotional excitement. And it says that the experience of beauty is the best means of achieving this "quickened sense of life," "this fruit of a quickened, multiplied consciousness." It enables one "to burn always with a hard, gemlike flame," and so to attain success in life.

Such an emphasis on intensity can easily lead astray. To be sure, the idea was not a new one in the history of English criticism.[1] Hobbes had originated the theory in England that agitation, motion, is the beginning of delight.[2] We feel definite pleasure when the mind is stirred from its lethargy and put in an active state. Eighteenth-century writers, such as Dennis, Addison, Akenside, Gildon, and Hume, accepted this, and used it as basis for the further belief that poetry is delightful because it rouses the mind. This became a fundamental part of the romantic tradition, leading to such arguments as Colcridge's in behalf of the drama as a means of arousing men from lethargy.[3] Hazlitt speaks of the high happiness and intel-

[1] The development of the idea is outlined in an unpublished manuscript read by Professor Clarence D. Thorpe, Un. of Michigan, at a meeting of the MLA, Dec. 1934.

[2] *The Elements of Law* (ed. F. Tönnies, Cambridge, 1928), pt. I, ch. 7, pp. 21–4.

[3] *Lectures upon Shakespeare*, Works (ed. W. G. T. Shedd, New York, 1853), IV, 45.

lectual excitement the painter finds in his work,[1] and says, "Why the excitement of intellectual activity pleases, is not here the question; but that it does so, is a general and acknowledged law of the human mind." [2] Allied to this was an emphasis on the power of art to move the emotions. The neo-classics valued that power, though they did not often, it seems to us, attain it in their works. The romantics made it a fundamental part of their theory. The truth expressed in poetry, said Wordsworth in a characteristic passage, is "carried alive into the heart by passion." [3]

But to cherish art because it stimulates intellectual excitement and arouses the emotions is not enough. By itself such an attitude may easily lead, as it did with the more extreme romantics, to an enjoyment of the exaggerated, even the morbid, and to a disregard of the further values which art can provide. The neo-classics had been in no danger of this particular error. Believing that art should both please and instruct, they had put so much emphasis on instruction that they all too often fell into a didactic strain. The greater of the romantics maintained a wise balance. Their critic spokesmen taught that while the first aim of art is to give pleasure, it has as an important result an enlarging effect, a kind of fertilizing of the mind. We shall see that Pater soon followed them. But when he wrote the various essays collected in the *Renaissance,* he was still immature. He had not yet acquired balance of spirit nor of doctrine. In speaking of art for the

[1] "On the Pleasure of Painting," *Table Talk,* Complete Works (ed. P. P. Howe, London, 1930), VIII, 11.

[2] "On Imitation," *The Round Table,* Works, IV, 75.

[3] Wordsworth, Preface to the *Lyrical Ballads,* Prose Works (ed. Wm. Knight, London, 1896), I, 59.

sake of the full life, he sometimes meant art for the sake of sheer intensity.

This is only one element in the *Renaissance,* however. If we search further, we find that he cherishes many of the deeper ethical values which art may bring. His main points are always essentially humane. Leonardo, he thinks, was attempting to penetrate into the inmost secrets of nature and the human soul; Botticelli was able, because of his great sympathy for frail mankind, to "convey into his work something more than is usual of the true complexion of humanity"; Pico della Mirandola represented the generous attempt of Renaissance philosophy to take up into Christian theology all that was good in Greek religion; *Aucassin and Nicolette* embodied the claim of the Renaissance for the full play of human affection; the poetry of Michelangelo was composed in order to "tranquillize and sweeten" his vehement passions by idealizing them. Winckelmann is an example of the power of art in aiding man to attain unity with himself, in giving him "breadth, centrality, with blitheness and repose." The Greek art which Winckelmann so loved should be a stimulus to us of later days to seek unity with ourselves; and the art of today has a comparable value.

> What modern art has to do in the service of culture is so to rearrange the details of modern life, so to reflect it, that it may satisfy the spirit. And what does the spirit need in the face of modern life? The sense of freedom.[1]

We seem caught in a web of natural law which we are powerless to modify; but art can give us a sense of power and free-

[1] Pp. 230-1.

dom by showing characters entangled in the web of natural law, yet working out the entanglement nobly.[1]

Such a concern with the place of art in the whole scheme of human values, such a desire for the unity and poise which art can encourage, are a sound basis for criticism. They give rise to many passages of depth and insight the loss of which would be a real loss to our literature. Beneath the disturbing glitter of the *Renaissance,* its patter of "brilliant sins and exquisite amusements," lies a perception of the best. Watching Pater's development, we shall soon see the meretricious elements fall away, and the soundness stand forth clear.

2. ART AS THE EXPRESSION OF THE INDIVIDUAL

From beginning to end one element in Pater's theory of the function of art remained constant—his stress on individuality. He believed that art is a highly characteristic matter, an expression of the personality of its creator. This comes out clearly in the *Renaissance,* where he says of the works of Luca della Robbia:

> They bear the impress of a personal quality, a profound expressiveness, what the French call *intimité,* by which is meant some subtler sense of originality—the seal on a man's work of what is most inward and peculiar in his moods, and manner of apprehension: it is what we call *expression,* carried to its highest intensity of degree. That characteristic is rare in poetry, rarer still in art, rarest of all in the abstract art of sculpture; yet essentially, perhaps, it is the quality which alone

---

[1] This reflects Hegel's conception of reconciliation through conflict. See pp. 61–5 *infra* for further discussion of Hegel's influence on this essay.

makes work in the imaginative order really worth having at all.[1]

The same idea permeates his later work. A characteristic statement of the matter is found in the essay on *Style*:

> Literary art . . . like all art which is in any way imitative or reproductive of fact—form, or colour, or incident—is the representation of such fact as connected with soul, of a specific personality, in its preferences, its volition and power.[2]

So in discussing Greek sculpture, which we are accustomed to think abstract and impersonal, Pater speaks of it first as expressing the religious sentiment of the Greeks, and then as also revealing the personalities and individual characteristics of each artist.[3]

The interest in specific personality, the peculiar quality of the individual, comes in a straight line from the romantics. Pater himself makes the connection. He traces the beginnings of romanticism back to Rousseau, who said, "I am not made like any one else I have ever known: yet, if I am not better, at least I am different." [4] He sees as the special characteristic of the romantic and modern ages "a consciousness brooding with delight over itself." [5]

Pater's emphasis on the individual may also be partly derived from Goethe, to whom he often refers. In his early period, Goethe felt that true art is "characteristic," that is, the

---

[1] Pp. 71–2.

[2] *Appre.*, p. 10; see whole essay.

[3] "Beginnings of Greek Sculpture," *Greek Studies, passim*. See also "Du Bellay," *Ren.*, pp. 167, 172; "Wordsworth," *Appre., passim*; "Rossetti," *Appre.*, p. 206.

[4] "Postscript," *Appre.*, p. 252.

[5] "Winckelmann," *Ren.*, p. 211.

expression of an individual mind, even though it may not have the formal proportions of beauty.[1] Later he came to emphasize a more generalized type of art, with moderation, harmony, fine proportions, high ideals. He came to believe that art has developed three levels: simple imitation of nature; the expression of the artist's own personality rather than of nature; and the expression of the universal as found in the particular. The last level is the highest, and is represented by Greek art with its generalized character, its grace, refinement, nobility.[2] Pater certainly did not take over this aesthetic theory bodily, but it is more than likely that he absorbed some of Goethe's belief in the importance of the individual. One of the latter's main ideas was that the artist must labor to make himself a full, rich personality, since his work is inevitably an expression of himself.

> If I were to say what I have been to the Germans in general and to the young poets in particular, I might perhaps call myself their liberator, for through me they have become aware that, as man must live from within outwards, so the artist must work from within outwards, seeing that, do what he will, he can only bring to light his own individuality.[3]

However much Pater may owe in this respect to the romantics in general and to Goethe in particular, his emphasis on the individual mind is even more a product of nineteenth-century philosophy, so strongly colored by science. He states his

[1] See his *Von deutscher Baukunst.*
[2] See *Einfache Nachahmung der Natur, Manier, Stil*; and *Der Sammler und die Seinigen.*
[3] "Noch ein Wort für junge Dichter," Werke, XXXVIII, 325. See also *supra,* p. 21.

28

own position in his first critical essay, *Coleridge's Writings.*
"Modern thought is distinguished from ancient by its cultiva-
tion of the 'relative spirit' in place of the 'absolute'." The
sciences of observation have developed this conception for us,
revealing "types of life evanescing into each other by inexpressible refinements of change." Now the task of the seeker
after truth is the "continual analysis of facts of rough and general observation into groups of facts more precise and minute.
The faculty for truth is recognized as a power of distinguishing and fixing delicate and fugitive detail." [1] Here Pater is,
like the scientists, a seeker after truths, rather than a seeker
after *the* truth, one and complete.

This position he himself sharply opposes to that of Coleridge, who believed in an absolute ideal, a super-sensible essence, which the artist's mind can detect as it manifests itself
in nature. Coleridge and the romantic philosophers, he says,
thought that knowledge of the natural world "is to be attained,
not by observation, experiment, analysis, patient generalisa-
tion, but by the evolution or recovery of those ideas directly
from within, by a sort of Platonic 'recollection'; every group
of observed facts remaining an enigma until the appropriate
idea is struck upon them from the mind of a Newton, or a
Cuvier, the genius in whom sympathy with the universal rea-

---

[1] *Appre.,* pp. 66–7. This appeared first in the *Westminster Review,*
LXXXV (Jan. 1866), 106–32. Pater took a large part of it later, made
slight alterations, and combined it with another sketch (originally written
as introduction to Coleridge's poems in Ward's *English Poets,* 1880) to
make the essay printed in *Appreciations.* The portion of the early article
omitted in this combination has been reprinted in *Sketches and Reviews*
under the title "Coleridge as Theologian." In quoting the *Westminster
Review* material, page references will be given as far as possible to *Appreciations,* since that is most readily accessible.

son becomes entire." [1] But Pater, through his whole life, is unwilling to accept an absolute. He does not deny that there may be such a thing, but he is sure that it is futile to theorize about it, because it is completely outside the reach of human knowledge—"to the modern spirit nothing is, or can be rightly known, except relatively and under conditions." [2] And so he cuts himself off from all transcendental philosophy. To him, art is always the sensuous representation of individual thought and feeling, but not of any absolute idea.

He is allying himself with the modern scientific spirit as he understands it. One phase of his thought echoes the conclusions of Herbert Spencer, [3] though it contains also a figure of speech perhaps borrowed from Bacon. [4]

> Our knowledge is limited to what we feel. . . . But can we be sure that things are at all like our feelings? Mere peculiarities in the instruments of our cognition, like the little knots and waves on the surface of a mirror, may distort the

[1] *Ibid.,* p. 77. (Commenting on the discovery of the possibilities for power in steam by the Marquis of Worcester, Coleridge points out that such a discovery did not occur by chance; it was reserved "for the genial spirit, that *saw* what it had been *seeking,* and saw *because* it sought. . . . When the bodily organ, steadying itself on some chance thing, imitates, as it were, the fixture of the 'inward eye' on its ideal shapings, then it is that Nature not seldom reveals her close affinity with mind. . . . Then it is, that Nature, like an individual spirit or fellow-soul, seems to think and hold commune with us." *Lectures upon Shakespeare,* Works, IV, 429.)

[2] *Ibid.,* p. 66.

[3] See Spencer's *Principles of Psychology* (2nd ed., 1872), I, pt. II, ch. III ("The Relativity of Feelings"), and ch. IV ("The Relativity of Relations between Feelings").

[4] "For the mind of man is far from the nature of a clear and equal glass, wherein the beams of things should reflect according to their true incidence; nay, it is rather like an enchanted glass, full of superstition and imposture." *Advancement of Learning* (ed. Wm. A. Wright, Oxford, 1920), II, pt. 14, § 9. Pater explicitly refers to Bacon two pages later: "*idola,* idols, false appearances, as Bacon calls them." (*Marius,* I, 141.)

matter they seem but to represent. Of other people we cannot truly know even the feelings. . . .

Pater, however, carries the train of reasoning along to a conclusion of his own:

> But our own impressions! . . . How reassuring, after so long a debate about the rival *criteria* of truth, to fall back upon direct sensation, to limit one's aspirations after knowledge to that![1]

If we can never know the thing-in-itself, nor even other people's opinions and feelings about it, what we must do in a work of art is to reproduce our own direct impressions of the world. Truth to the artist's own sense of fact, therefore, is the fundamental in art.

> In the highest as in the lowliest literature, then, the one indispensable beauty is, after all, truth:—truth to bare fact in the latter, as to some personal sense of fact, diverted somewhat from men's ordinary sense of it, in the former; truth there as accuracy, truth here as expression, that finest and most intimate form of truth, the *vraie vérité*.[2]

This general theory is very similar to the aesthetic philosophy of Eugène Véron, set forth in France a few years later.[3] Taine had talked about art as determined by environment—the race, the milieu, the moment. Véron reacted violently against this interpretation, saying that it left out of account the individual genius of the author, which after all was the determining factor in his work. If Véron had known Pater's critical writings,

---

[1] *Marius,* I, 138–9.
[2] "Style," *Appre.*, p. 34; see also whole essay.
[3] *Aesthetics,* trs. by W. H. Armstrong, London, 1879, a year after its first publication in France.

he could hardly have failed to see in them as in those of Sainte-Beuve an application of his own aesthetic theory, which held the individual to be much more important than the "moral temperature" of his time.

It is illuminating to watch Pater's reactions to the idea of certain French authors that an artist's style should be impersonal. Most of the writers of *l'art pour l'art* held this theory—Gautier, Flaubert, Banville, Leconte de Lisle, Heredia, and to a certain extent Baudelaire. Leconte de Lisle says, for instance, of his own poems:

> Les émotions personelles n'y ont laissé que peu de traces. . . . Bien que l'art puisse donner, dans une certain mesure, un caractère de généralité à tout ce qu'il touche, il y a dans l'aveu public des angoisses du cœur et de ses voluptés non moins amères, une vanité et une profanation gratuites.[1]

We find no trace of an acquaintance with this doctrine of impersonality in Pater till after he has read Flaubert's *Correspondance,* which says repeatedly that "Dans l'art, la passion ne fait pas les vers, et plus vous serez personnel, plus vous serez faible." [2] In his essay on *Style,* written in the same year as his first review of Flaubert's *Correspondance,* and with constant reference to that writer, Pater has apparently been swung over to the French view. He pronounces agreement with Flaubert, though he does not make his reasoning clear: "If the style be the man, in all the colour and intensity of a veritable apprehension, it will be in a real sense 'impersonal'." [3]

But this is only a tentative experiment with a new idea. In

---

[1] Préface des *Poèmes antiques,* reprinted in *Derniers poèmes,* 1895.
[2] (Paris, 1900), II, 82; see also pp. 75, 76–7.
[3] *Appre.,* p. 37.

his review of the second half of Flaubert's *Correspondance* a year later, he says, "Impersonality in art, the literary ideal of Gustave Flaubert, is perhaps no more possible than realism. The artist *will* be felt; his subjectivity must and will colour the incidents, as his very bodily eye *selects* the aspects of things." [1] A year later still, he is again occupied with the question of "Personality *versus* impersonality in art:—how much or how little of one's self one may put into one's work: . . . whether one *can* put there anything else." [2] And his conclusion is, emphatically, no. Flaubert tried to be impersonal but often failed. Mérimée seemed to succeed. And yet his "superb self-effacement, his impersonality, is itself but an effective personal trait, and, transferred to art, becomes a markedly peculiar quality of literary beauty." [3]

Though this emphasis on the personal, individual quality of each artist's work is a natural outgrowth of romanticism and of nineteenth-century philosophy, no English critic before Pater had carried it as far as he. While the romantic critics had shown a great interest in the psychological workings of the mind of the artist and of the observer, they had still held up as their main standard of judgment truth to universal human nature. Coleridge, for instance, the critic who delved most profoundly into the workings of the mind, emphasized over and over again the creative power of the imagination, and the fact that the artist's mind shapes and forms the material presented him by nature.[4] But he also insisted that "a faith-

[1] *Sketches and Reviews,* pp. 79–80.
[2] "Mérimée," *Misc. Studies,* p. 35.
[3] *Ibid.,* p. 37.
[4] *Biographia Literaria* (ed. J. Shawcross, Oxford, 1907), I, 107, 202; "Definition of Poetry," Works, IV, 19–22.

ful adherence to the truth of nature" was the aim.[1] Shakespeare "first conceived what the forms of things must be and then went humbly to the oracle of nature to ask whether he was right." [2] And he did not write from the human nature peculiar to himself, but as a representative of universal human nature. "Shakespeare shaped his characters out of the nature within; but we cannot so safely say, out of his own nature as an individual person. No! . . . Shakespeare, in composing, had no I, but the I representative." [3]

All through the nineteenth century the same demand had been made—truth to nature. Ruskin had been particularly insistent on it, and so had the Pre-Raphaelites in their theories of painting. But in Swinburne's early work the emphasis had been much diminished; and now in Pater, we find it largely replaced by the stress on truth to the individuality of the artist. Oscar Wilde was soon to take the one remaining step, and declare that art did not even pretend to be true to nature; that, on the contrary, "Art is our spirited protest, our gallant attempt to teach Nature her proper place." [4] Far from Art's imitating Nature, Nature endeavors to form itself on Art. "Where, if not from the Impressionists, do we get those wonderful brown fogs that come creeping down our streets, blurring the gas-lamps and changing the houses into monstrous

---

[1] *Biog. Lit.*, II, 5.

[2] *Coleridge's Shakespearean Criticism* (ed. T. M. Raysor, London, 1930), II, 17.

[3] *Lectures on Shakespeare*, Works, IV, 257. Cf. Wordsworth: "Aristotle, I have been told, has said, that poetry is the most philosophic of all writing: it is so: its object is truth, not individual and local, but general, and operative." Preface to the *Lyrical Ballads*, Prose Works, I, 59.

[4] "The Decay of Lying," *Intentions*, Works (ed. R. Ross, Boston, 1909), III, 4.

shadows?" [1] "The nineteenth century, as we know it, is largely an invention of Balzac." [2]

Pater of course did not go to this extreme, extremes of any kind being foreign to his nature. His work, in fact, presupposes not only differences among individual temperaments, but also a substratum of human nature common to all. This is implicit throughout the *Renaissance,* as for instance when he praises Michelangelo for giving us the "austere truths of human nature," [3] and characterizes Abelard's story as an assertion of the claims of the "free play of human affection," [4] and "the free play of human intelligence around all subjects presented to it." [5] It is explicit in the essay on Winckelmann, which says that Greek sculpture "unveils man in the repose of his unchanging characteristics." [6]

The recognition of the common elements of human nature becomes more emphatic in Pater's later work, appearing particularly in the essay on *The Marbles of Aegina,* and in his anonymous book reviews. Doric art, he thinks, embodied the religion of Apollo, which was "a sanction of, and an encouragement towards the true valuation of humanity, in its sanity, its proportion, its knowledge of itself." [7] Thus inspired, the Greeks gave us sculpture "which bears upon it the full expression of this humanism,"—the marbles of Aegina,

> a work, in which the presence of man, realized with complete mastery of hand, and with clear apprehension of how he actually is and moves and looks, is touched with the freshest sense of that new-found, inward value; the energy of worthy

[1] *Ibid.,* p. 41.
[2] *Ibid.,* p. 36.
[3] P. 77.
[4] P. 8.
[5] Pp. 3–4.
[6] P. 213.
[7] *Greek Studies,* p. 255.

passions purifying, the light of his reason shining through, bodily forms and motions, solemnised, attractive, pathetic.[1]

The *Greek Studies* are full of such recognitions of the universal.

The book reviews also are full of similar implications. Of *Robert Elsmere,* Pater says that it presents "no mere flighty remnants, but . . . typical forms, of character, firmly and fully conceived." [2] And he admires Browning because his chosen subject matter is "the individual, the personal, the concrete, as distinguished from, yet revealing in its fulness, the general, the universal." [3] In one of the late criticisms, an introduction to Shadwell's *Dante,* he calls Dante "great like Sophocles and Shakespeare by a certain universality in his appeal to men's minds, and independent therefore of the special sensibilities of a particular age." [4]

Pater's interest in the formal aspects of beauty implies a recognition of common qualities in the human mind. He bases his demand for unity and structure on the constitution of the human spirit, which possesses order and harmony, and requires the same from art. Both in *Style* and the essay on Mérimée, he specifies *mind* as "the quality which secures flawless literary structure," in combination with *soul,* which secures a finer and more subtle unity, not of structure but of atmosphere.[5]

Pater's conception of art has also room for the theory which sees art as representing an age or an epoch. After all, the artist

---

[1] *Ibid.,* pp. 256–7.
[2] *Guardian,* p. 56.
[3] *Guardian,* p. 44.
[4] *Uncollected Essays,* p. 156.
[5] "Mérimée,"*Misc. Studies,* p. 37; "Style," *Appre.,* pp. 21–7.

is the child of his time, and his view of life will inevitably be colored by the period in which he lives.

> That ages have their genius as well as the individual; that in every age there is a peculiar *ensemble* of conditions which determines a common character in every product of that age, in business and art, in fashion and speculation, in religion and manners, in men's very faces; that nothing man has projected from himself is really intelligible except at its own date, and from its proper point of view in the never-resting "secular process"; . . . by force of these convictions many a normal, or at first sight abnormal, phase of speculation has found a reasonable meaning for us.[1]

It is necessary for the scholar still to remember that "if 'the style is the man' it is also the age." [2]

Pater attributes this conception of the "nimbly-shifting *Time-Spirit,* or *Zeit-Geist,*" particularly to Hegel,[3] and calls it "only one of the applications, the most fruitful of them all, of the relative spirit." [4] He may well have had Taine in mind also when he says that it is "understood by French not less than by German criticism." [5] And he adopts it himself in place after place, as when he calls Coleridge a representative of his own times, displaying the modern romantic temper with its "inexhaustible discontent, languor, and homesickness, that endless regret." [6]

In short, though Pater admits no Absolute which art is to

---

[1] *Plato and Platonism,* pp. 9–10.
[2] "Postscript," *Appre.,* p. 261.
[3] *Plato and Platonism,* p. 9.
[4] "Coleridge's Writings," *Westminster Rev.,* LXXXV, 129.
[5] "Postscript," *Appre.,* p. 256.
[6] "Coleridge," *Appre.,* p. 104.

express, and though he lays more emphasis than any important English critic before him on art as expressing the individuality of the particular creator, his theory has place also for art as representing the spirit of an age or period, and the elements common to human nature. These conceptions were already well developed in the *Renaissance,* and extended throughout his work.

3. ART AS ENLARGING AND ENNOBLING THE MIND

The *Studies in the History of the Renaissance* was published in 1873. In the next year appeared the essay on Wordsworth, the work, one might almost think, of a different person. Whereas in the first Pater had written of delicate comeliness, strange beauty, art for art's sake, in the *Wordsworth* his tone had deepened and strengthened. He spoke now of a poet's sense of the moral and spiritual life in nature, his understanding of the deepest passions of man, his enforcing the lessons of a life of contemplation and of life as an end in itself. This deeper tone pervaded all of Pater's subsequent work. He turned at once to a series of *Greek Studies* which dealt with the art of the Greeks as it sprang from and embodied religious conceptions. And he set himself to show, through an account of a Roman youth, *Marius the Epicurean,* what he himself had really meant by the misleading Conclusion to the *Renaissance* and what his development had been since that was written.

In harmony with this deeper tone in Pater's mature work, we can trace an actual development in his aesthetic. It is clear in the essay on Wordsworth that he is now taking up into his theory some of the conceptions of the function of art common

38

The Function of Art

to the English romantic critics.[1] Such romantics as Wordsworth, Coleridge, Lamb, Hazlitt, and Shelley had gone further than merely cherishing art because it stirs the mind and arouses the emotions. They had believed that this arousing has a far-reaching, beneficial, almost moral effect. Wordsworth is fairly representative of their doctrine in saying that a great poet "ought, to a certain degree, to rectify men's feelings, to give them new compositions of feeling, to render their feelings more sane, pure, and permanent."[2] Poetry, he declares elsewhere, enlightens the understanding of the reader and strengthens and purifies his affections.[3] Shelley is even more successful in defining this ethical function of art when he says that poetry

> awakens and enlarges the mind itself by rendering it the receptacle of a thousand unapprehended combinations of thought. . . . The great secret of morals is love. . . . A man, to be greatly good, must imagine intensely and comprehensively; he must put himself in the place of another and of many others; the pains and pleasures of his species must become his own. . . . Poetry strengthens that faculty which is the organ of the moral nature of man, in the same manner as exercise strengthens a limb.[4]

Pater is, regrettably, much less interested in the psychology of the aesthetic experience than were the romantic critics in general, and gives comparatively little space to its considera-

---

[1] Pater's first published essay had been on Coleridge, but in it he indicates a lack of sympathy with Coleridge, rather than an adoption of his ideas. *Westminster Rev.*, LXXXV (Jan. 1866), pp. 106–32.

[2] Letter to Wilson, Prose Works, I, 39.

[3] Preface to *Lyrical Ballads,* Prose Works, I, 50.

[4] "Defence of Poetry," Complete Works (ed. R. Ingpen and W. E. Peck, London, 1930), VII, 117–8.

tion. But he does come in his more mature period to insist with them that the stimulation which art provides has a morally beneficial effect. "The office of the poet is not that of the moralist," he says, "and the first aim of Wordsworth's poetry is to give the reader a peculiar kind of pleasure. But through his poetry, and through this pleasure in it, he does actually convey to the reader an extraordinary wisdom in the things of practice."[1] Wordsworth chooses pastoral settings for his poems, not because of their passionless calm, but because they give a clear background for the "almost elementary expression of elementary feelings." "And so he has much for those who value highly the concentrated presentment of passion, who appraise men and women by their susceptibility to it, and art and poetry as they afford the spectacle of it."[2] Thus he teaches us, as do all great artists, the proper attitude toward life, that is, the attitude of impassioned contemplation. He withdraws our thoughts from the mere machinery of life and fixes them on the passions and doings of men and on the world of nature. "To witness this spectacle with appropriate emotions is the aim of all culture; and of these emotions poetry like Wordsworth's is a great nourisher and stimulant."[3] Wordsworth himself, we may object, would hardly have gone so far as to say that witnessing the spectacle of life with appropriate emotions was the aim of all culture.[4] But the romantic

[1] "Wordsworth," *Appre.*, p. 59.
[2] *Ibid.*, p. 52.
[3] *Ibid.*, p. 63.
[4] Cf., however, Wordsworth's statement: "The human mind is capable of being excited without the application of gross and violent stimulants; and he must have a very faint perception of its beauty and dignity who does not know this, and who does not further know that one being is elevated above another, in proportion as he possesses this capability. It has

40

The Function of Art

idea of the importance of art in moving the emotions has now become one of the cornerstones of Pater's gradually developing conception of life.[1]

From the time of the *Wordsworth* on, Pater recognizes the ethical value of art in its effect on the mind and heart. The end of his essay on *Measure for Measure* is a very close parallel to the passage quoted above from Shelley. He praises that difficult play because it sympathetically presents the essence of each character, and so develops in us a yearning to see poetic justice done to each. As true justice springs from an understanding of what each person really is, its essence is "a finer knowledge through love."

> It is not always that poetry can be the exponent of morality; but it is this aspect of morals which it represents most naturally, for this true justice is dependent on just those finer appreciations which poetry cultivates in us the power of making, those peculiar valuations of action and its effect which poetry actually requires.[2]

Again, he says that romantic literature in France reaches a genuine pathos; "for the habit of noting and distinguishing one's own most intimate passages of sentiment makes one sympathetic, begetting, as it must, the power of entering, by all sorts of finer ways, into the intimate recesses of other minds; so that pity is another quality of romanticism." [3]

Putting these remarks together, we see that the habit of

---

therefore appeared to me, that to endeavor to produce or enlarge this capability is one of the best services in which, at any period, a Writer can be engaged." Preface to *Lyrical Ballads,* Prose Works, I, 52.
[1] For further discussion of this point, see *infra,* pp. 80–1, 101.
[2] *Appre.,* p. 184.
[3] "Postscript," *Appre.,* p. 254.

noting one's own "most intimate passages of sentiment" creates in one understanding and sympathy for other people; and that when this is expressed in art, as it is in *Measure for Measure,* it arouses in turn a power of understanding and sympathy on the part of the beholder. It conducts one to "an exquisite appreciation of all the finer traits of nature and of man." [1] In line with this idea, Pater praises Lamb for having "reached an enduring moral effect also, in a sort of boundless sympathy"; he sees in him a gift for appreciating the pathos of small things in life, and "a gift also for the enjoyment of life in its subtleties." [2]

Pater's last book, *Plato and Platonism,* is particularly filled with implications that beauty has an ethical value. He praises Plato's *Republic,* in which "the connexion between moral character and matters of poetry and art" is "strongly asserted," and says that Plato recognizes the "close connexion between what may be called the aesthetic qualities of the world about us and the formation of moral character, between aesthetics and ethics." [3]

Coalescing with the theory that art has an ethical value is Pater's growing emphasis on the ideal. This, as his work matures, becomes all-pervasive, and gathers up everything else into itself. It had been present to some extent, though not clearly explained, in the *Renaissance.* There he speaks occasionally of the ideality of art, and tells us that "the basis of all artistic genius lies in the power of conceiving humanity in a new and striking way, of putting a happy world of its own creation in place of the meaner world of our common days." [4] Very

[1] *Marius,* I, 147.
[2] *Appre.,* pp. 109–10.
[3] P. 269.
[4] "Winckelmann," *Ren.,* p. 213.

early he had said that "Greek poetry, medieval or modern poetry, projects, above the realities of its time, a world in which the forms of things are transfigured." [1] But it is not till the *Greek Studies,* of which the first appeared the year after *Wordsworth,* that the conception of the ideal appears constantly. In *Marius the Epicurean* it reaches its full scope.

As we study Pater's mature work we find that this conception has several aspects. Often he uses the word 'ideal' in its most common meaning of 'the perfect model,' Rossetti being, for instance, the poet of "the ideal intensity of love," and Plato writing about the "ideal city," or the "ideal state." [2] But often he uses it in much more individual fashion, equating it with the 'type.' He calls the mythical death of Semele in childbirth, for instance, "a sort of ideal or type of this peculiar claim on human pity," [3] and speaks of music as "the typical, or ideally consummate art." [4] Evidently he is not using the word 'typical' in its ordinary sense. And so we are pleased to find that later he defines for us 'typical.' Of the *Discobolus* he inquires,

Was it the portrait of one much-admired youth, or rather the type, the rectified essence, of many such, at the most pregnant, the essential, moment, of the exercise of their natural powers, of what they really were? Have we here, in short, the sculptor Myron's reasoned memory of many a quoit-player, of a long flight of quoit-players; as, were he here, he might have given us the cricketer, the passing gen-

---

[1] "Aesthetic Poetry," *Sketches and Reviews,* p. 1; see also p. 2.
[2] In only a few instances he uses the word to mean the "abstract thought" as opposed to its "sensible vehicle or occasion." See "Child in the House," *Misc. Studies,* p. 186, and "Marbles of Aegina," *Greek Studies,* p. 251.
[3] "Dionysus," *Greek Studies,* pp. 44–5.
[4] "Giorgione," *Ren.,* pp. 134–5.

eration of cricketers, *sub specie eternitatis,* under the eternal form of art? [1]

This conception of the ideal as the purified essence or type is like that of Ruskin, who defined it, in very similar fashion, as "the noble generic form which indicates the full perfection of the creature in all its functions." [2]

The beautiful representation in which the ideal or essence is conveyed, Pater calls the 'spiritual form' of the object. Here he says he is borrowing an expression from William Blake, and explains it thus: "form, with hands, and lips, and opened eyelids—spiritual, as conveying to us, in that, the soul of rain, or of a Greek river, or of swiftness, or purity." [3] Pan and his children are "the *spiritual form* of Arcadia, and the ways of human life there," its "reflexion, in sacred image or ideal." [4] The essays on Greek myth and sculpture repeatedly use the expressions 'spiritual form' and 'ideal.' Of none of them is this more true than of the *Age of Athletic Prizemen,* which was published in the last year of his life.

Pater gives a psychological explanation of the mode of arriving at the ideal or typical in his lectures on *Plato and Platonism.* He takes his own stand, he says, "somewhere between the realist and the conceptualist."

There is a general consciousness, a permanent common sense, independent indeed of each one of us, but with which we are, each one of us, in communication. It is in that, those common or general ideas really reside. And we might add

[1] "Athletic Prizemen," *Greek Studies,* pp. 289–90; see also p. 281.
[2] *Modern Painters,* II, pt. III, sec. 1, ch. 13, § 4, Works, IV, 167; see also § 12–14, pp. 172–5.
[3] "Dionysus," *Greek Studies,* p. 37.
[4] *Ibid.,* p. 15.

just here (giving his due to the nominalist also) that those abstract or common notions come to the individual mind through language, through common or general names, *Animal, Justice, Equality,* into which one's individual experience, little by little, drop by drop, conveys their full meaning or content; and, by the instrumentality of such terms and notions, thus locating the particular in the general, mediating between general and particular, between our individual experience and the common experience of our kind, we come to understand each other, and to assist each other's thoughts, as in a common mental atmosphere, an 'intellectual world,' . . . So much for the modern view; for what common sense might now suggest as to the nature of logical 'universals.' [1]

Here Pater shows himself a modified Platonist. The imaginative mind is able to construct out of the many individual objects a typical, ideal object. But that ideal is not transcendental for him, as it was for Plato, and for the long succession of Neo-Platonists. It is constructed by the power of the artist's own mind out of experience, and the observation of many particulars.

The ideal of which Pater speaks reminds one somewhat of the old neo-classic conception, excellently summed up by Dryden in his *Parallel between Poetry and Painting.* Dryden quotes first from the Italian critic, Bellori, giving a history of the ideal as conceived by Cicero, Lysippus, Seneca, Alberti, Da Vinci, Raphael, and others. Then he sums it up in his own words:

A learned painter should form to himself an idea of perfect nature. This image he is to set before his mind in all his

[1] Pp. 151–2.

45

undertakings, and to draw from thence, as from a store-house, the beauties which are to enter into his work; thereby correcting nature from what actually she is in individuals, to what she ought to be, and what she was created.[1]

But Pater's ideal is unlike the neo-classic in several particulars. It does not involve the Platonic element of ideal form in the mind of the artist; nor the influence of the study of classic works in forming the ideal; nor the element of deliberate selection of the itemized best features which are to be combined to make the beautiful object.

Nor is Pater's an idea borrowed from the romantic critics of the early nineteenth century. To be sure, they had occasionally used the term "idealizing power" to describe that function of the mind on which they put so much emphasis, its ability to abstract from experience and to create an imaginative reality of its own out of the fleeting impressions of the world. But this imaginative reality was "ideal" in the sense of being an idea, rather than in Pater's usual sense of being the idea of a perfection. In any other sense than this, few had concerned themselves much with the problem of the ideal. Hazlitt is one of the few to give it attention, using the term to mean beauty characterized by the symmetry and harmony which the mind craves, as higher than the merely picturesque or striking.[2] Shelley is the romantic writer who affords the closest similarity to Pater, for he, too, constantly stresses the ideal or perfect beauty which art presents. But he holds the neo-Platonic belief in "the unchangeable forms of human nature, as exist-

[1] Works (ed. Scott and Saintsbury, London, 1892), XVII, 300.
[2] *Table Talk,* Works, VIII, 320; see also his "On the Ideal" (Works, XVIII, 82–3), and "On Beauty" (*Round Table,* Works, IV, 68–72).

ing in the mind of the Creator, which is itself the image of all other minds," and says that poetry presents to us these divine forms directly, without the distortion they regularly receive in their earthly embodiments.[1] And he emphasizes the identification of beauty with truth and goodness.

To the vision of the ideal Pater looks increasingly for the value of art. Human nature, he tells us, has a constant longing for ideal perfection.[2] But the world of daily living appears mean and sordid, and does not satisfy our souls. We therefore grasp at various means of escaping from it, and lifting ourselves above its sordid aspects.[3] Art is perhaps the best means of escape. It affords us "a refuge into a world slightly better— better conceived, or better finished—than the real one." [4]

> All disinterested lovers of books, will always look to it [literature], as to all other fine art, for a refuge, a sort of cloistral refuge, from a certain vulgarity in the actual world. A perfect poem like *Lycidas,* a perfect fiction like *Esmond,* the perfect handling of a theory like Newman's *Idea of a University,* has for them something of the uses of a religious 'retreat.' [5]

This sounds very much like Bacon's idea of poetry as "feigned history," whose purpose is to satisfy man's longing for that greatness, goodness, and variety which can be found in no satisfactory measure in the nature of things: "Therefore it was ever thought to have some participation of divineness, be-

---

[1] "The Defence of Poetry," *Works,* VII, 115.
[2] *Marius,* I, 98.
[3] For the position of this idea in Pater's philosophy of life, see *infra,* pp. 101–5.
[4] "Feuillet's *La Morte,*" *Appre.,* p. 219.
[5] "Style," *Appre.,* p. 18.

cause it doth raise and erect the mind, by submitting the shows of things to the desires of the mind; whereas reason doth buckle and bow the mind unto the nature of things." [1]

We may inquire whether Pater's two conceptions of the ideal outlined above are consistent—an ideal world better than the real one into which we may escape; and a world of typical objects constructed by the creative mind out of a knowledge of countless individual instances. Logically speaking, they do not fit together, for the essence or type of some ugly portion of life would not afford us an attractive escape. The racketeer is as much a type as the *Discobolus*. But the conceptions are psychologically, if not logically, compatible. Idealists have always tended to believe that ugliness is a distortion of reality, a failure to achieve the essence. Plato and Aristotle in their very different ways were agreed on this, and so were all the neo-Platonic thinkers down through such nineteenth-century representatives as Coleridge and Shelley.

Professor George Santayana has given a very excellent psychological explanation, in *The Sense of Beauty*, of exactly the mental process by which a modern thinker like Pater may easily arrive at this double view of the ideal. He starts from the same point as Pater, that a type is a residuum of experience; it holds our past associations with the members of the type. But he goes on to say that the "percepts" we build up are of course biased.

> Not all parts of an object are equally congruous with our perceptive faculty; not all elements are noted with the same pleasure. Those, therefore, which are agreeable are chiefly dwelt upon by the lover of beauty, and his percept will give

[1] *Advancement of Learning*, II, pt. 4, § 2.

48

an average of things with a great emphasis laid on that part of them which is beautiful. The ideal will thus deviate from the average in the direction of the observer's pleasure.

For this reason the world is so much more beautiful to a poet or an artist than to an ordinary man. Each object, as his aesthetic sense is developed, is perhaps less beautiful than to the uncritical eye. . . . But while each work of nature and art is thus apparently blighted by his greater demands and keener susceptibility, the world itself, and the various natures it contains, are to him unspeakably beautiful. . . . Criticism and idealization involve each other. . . . Many imperfect things crystallize into a single perfection. The mind is thus peopled by general ideas in which beauty is the chief quality; and these ideas are at the same time the types of things. The type is still a natural resultant of particular impressions; but the formation of it has been guided by a deep subjective bias in favor of what has delighted the eye.[1]

Here we have the explanation of Pater's combination-theory of the ideal. We see how his longing to escape from vulgar reality could find its satisfaction in building up an ideal out of the vulgar, in seeing the ideal significance of the real.[2]

The ideal in art, however, does much more than merely allow us to vanish for a while from our unsatisfactory world into a delightful one. It sums up for us the quintessence of life.

It is part of the ideality of the highest sort of dramatic poetry, that it presents us with a kind of profoundly signifi-

[1] Pp. 122–3 (New York, 1896).
[2] For other significant references to the ideal, see "Michelangelo," *Ren.*, p. 86; "Giorgione," *Ren.*, p. 141; "A Prince of Court Painters," *Imag. Por.*, pp. 5–6, 34–5; *Gaston*, pp. 54–5; "Amiel's Journal," *Guardian*, p. 34.

cant and animated instants, a mere gesture, a look, a smile, perhaps—some brief and wholly concrete moment—into which, however, all the motives, all the interests and effects of a long history, have condensed themselves, and which seem to absorb past and future in an intense consciousness of the present. Such ideal instants the school of Giorgione selects . . . exquisite pauses in time, in which, arrested thus, we seem to be spectators of all the fulness of existence, and which are like some consummate extract or quintessence of life.[1]

The ideal also ennobles our sentiments. At this point, beginning with the first of the *Greek Studies,* Pater's view of the ideal coalesces with his newly developed conception of art as purifying and strengthening the emotions. The statues of Demeter and Persephone, he says, "lend themselves to the elevation and correction of the sentiments of sorrow and awe, by the presentment to the senses and imagination of an ideal expression of them." [2] Watteau's pictures cast an unreal, imaginary light upon the scenes of life, and at the same time reveal its inherent poetry. The spectators are not only better off for that, but actually the better. For his art has "its care for purity, its cleanly preferences, in what one is to *see*," and so is "a sign, a memento, . . . of what makes life really valuable." [3] For Marius, the story of Cupid and Psyche, as he read it in the Golden Book, "served to combine many lines of meditation, already familiar to Marius, into the ideal of a perfect imaginative love, centered upon a type of beauty entirely flaw-

[1] "The School of Giorgione," *Ren.,* p. 150, published in 1877, inserted in 3rd ed. of *Ren.*
[2] "Demeter and Persephone," *Greek Studies,* p. 93.
[3] "A Prince of Court Painters," *Imag. Por.,* pp. 32–3.

less and clean—an ideal which never wholly faded from his thoughts, though he valued it at various times in different degrees." [1]

It is in *Marius* that Pater's philosophy of life reaches its full development. There, as we shall see later, the impassioned contemplation of the ideal is finally set forth as the essence of art, morality, and religion. And since works of art "present the most perfect forms of life—spirit and matter alike under their purest and most perfect conditions," they are "the most strictly appropriate objects of that impassioned contemplation." [2]

4. 'ART FOR ART'S SAKE' IN PATER'S LATER WORK

Pater has gradually attained a highly individual, almost mystical, conception of the function of art. And in the process the emphasis on art for art's sake has dropped back into a minor place. In general, the references to the idea have become more guarded. Lamb, Pater says, is a disinterested servant of literature, who "in the making of prose . . . realizes the principle of art for its own sake, as completely as Keats in the making of verse." [3] But in so doing, by working close to the concrete, "he has reached an enduring moral effect also, in a sort of boundless sympathy." [4] The praise of Rossetti is noncommittal as to Pater's own beliefs:

> Rossetti, indeed, with all his self-concentration upon his own peculiar aim, by no means ignored those general interests which are external to poetry as he conceived it. . . . It was but that, in a life to be shorter even than the average, he

[1] *Marius,* I, 92.　　　　　[3] *Appre.,* p. 109.
[2] I, 147–8. See *infra,* pp. 101–5.　[4] *Ibid.,* pp. 109–10.

found enough to occupy him in the fulfilment of a task, plainly 'given him to do.' [1]

As to Flaubert, Pater points out that he believed in "artistic detachment from all practical ends," and adds noncommittally, "Flaubert himself, whatever we may think of that, had certainly attained a remarkable degree of detachment from the ordinary interests of mankind." [2]

Some of Pater's latest utterances seem definitely hostile to the idea of art for art's sake. The incompleted fragment, *Gaston de Latour,* is in striking contrast to the *Renaissance* essay on Joachim du Bellay, which deals with the same period. In the early essay, Pater had praised the French of the sixteenth century for their love of art, which they treated with "elegance," an "aerial touch," a "perfect manner." [3] Now in *Gaston* he says that this same society was "somewhat distraught by an artificial aesthetic culture." [4] Ronsard, the great poet of the age, showed in his face "the haggard soul of a haggard generation, whose eagerly-sought refinements had been after all little more than a theatrical make-believe—an age of wild people, of insane impulse, of homicidal mania. The sweet-souled songster had no more than others attained real calm in it." [5]

A similar passage in *Mérimée* is even more definitely hostile to the idea of art for art's sake. There Pater reprobates the artist who turns to art with fanaticism as an end in itself, unrelated to life. He starts by defining the spirit of the nineteenth century as a reaction from the hopes of the French

---

[1] *Appre.,* pp. 217–18.
[2] *Sketches and Reviews,* p. 84.
[3] P. 158.
[4] P. 16.
[5] P. 67.

The Function of Art

Revolution, and of the Kantian philosophers, in the disillusion produced by the Empire and the progress of empirical science. In every department of action, principles once thought eternal had been withdrawn. Though disillusioned, the more energetic souls try to make the best of the situation, giving themselves to art, to the passions, and to science. They turn to

> art, or science, to the experience of life itself, not as to portions of human nature's daily food, but as to something that must be, by the circumstances of the case, exceptional; almost as men turn in despair to gambling or narcotics, and in a little while the narcotic, the game of chance or skill, is valued for its own sake. The vocation of the artist, of the student of life or books, will be realized with something—say! of fanaticism, as an end in itself, unrelated, unassociated.[1]

Consequently the art, passion, science, to which they turn will be exaggerated. This has been true in French literature: a passionate love of passion, with Balzac; an art exaggerated in form or matter or both, as with Hugo or Baudelaire.

The most famous presentation of Pater's later ideas comes at the end of the essay on *Style*. Here he makes the distinction between good art and great art depend immediately, not on the form, but on the matter:

> Thackeray's *Esmond*, surely, is greater art than *Vanity Fair*, by the greater dignity of its interests. It is on the quality of the matter it informs or controls, its compass, its variety, its alliance to great ends, or the depth of the note of revolt, or the largeness of hope in it, that the greatness of literary art depends, as *The Divine Comedy, Paradise Lost, Les Misérables, The English Bible,* are great art.

[1] *Misc. Studies,* pp. 12–3.

The Aesthetic of Walter Pater

And he goes on to say:

> Given the conditions I have tried to explain as constituting good art;—then, if it be devoted further to the increase of men's happiness, to the redemption of the oppressed, or the enlargement of our sympathies with each other, or to such presentment of new or old truth about ourselves and our relation to the world as may ennoble and fortify us in our sojourn here, or immediately, as with Dante, to the glory of God, it will be also great art; if, over and above those qualities I summed up as mind and soul—that colour and mystic perfume, and that reasonable structure, it has something of the soul of humanity in it, and finds its logical, its architectural place, in the great structure of human life.[1]

This is especially interesting as a reasoned statement of Pater's mature views on the matter, because it was written with Flaubert's *Correspondance* particularly in mind, and presumably represents Pater's reaction to the art for art's sake views as he found them presented there.[2]

However Pater may have changed and developed, we find him in his last book, *Plato and Platonism,* hailing Plato as a forerunner of "the modern notion that art as such has no end but its own perfection,—'art for art's sake.' "[3] But though he may still believe in art for art's sake in a certain sense, his view is no longer a one-sided, narrowly 'aesthetic' one. It has become wisely balanced, soundly proportioned. While he still rightly denies that art "as such" has any external moral or religious aim, he recognizes also that it does indeed accomplish an important ethical result in enlarging and orienting the soul.

[1] *Appre.,* p. 38.   [2] See *infra,* pp. 69–70.   [3] P. 268.

CHAPTER II

Formal Aspects of Art

I. THE RELATION BETWEEN CONTENT AND FORM

WE HAVE SEEN that Pater's idea of the function of art developed till it became distinctly different from the typical art for art's sake idea. In his emphasis on the importance of artistic form, however, he was unquestionably akin to the group of *l'art pour l'art*. In their single-minded devotion to beauty, these French writers considered form of absorbing importance. They demanded a high degree of conscious artistry, and thought no labor too arduous in the service of perfection. Lanson has happily named this "the categorical imperative of the artistic conscience." He sums up the movement thus: "Culte de la beauté, autonomie de l'artiste, *impératif catégorique* de la conscience artistique, voilà, me semble-t-il, le contenu essentiel de *l'art pour l'art*." [1] Pater felt that same categorical imperative. And yet he probably drew his ideas on the subject of form more from English and German sources than from French. His relation to the group of *l'art pour l'art* was a temperamental similarity rather than a discipleship.

'Identity of form and content' was Pater's own particular phrasing for an idea generally accepted in the nineteenth century—the idea that form and content must be so completely fused as to be one indivisible unit. The English romantic crit-

[1] *Revue d'histoire littéraire de la France,* XIV (1907), 167.

ics, impelled by the need for defending Shakespeare's irregular workmanship, had adopted a doctrine of organic form. In discussing Shakespeare, Coleridge says:

> The form is mechanic, when on any given material we impress a predetermined form, not necessarily arising out of the properties of the material;—as when to a mass of wet clay we give whatever shape we wish it to retain when hardened. The organic form, on the other hand, is innate; it shapes, as it develops, itself from within, and the fulness of its development is one and the same with the perfection of its outward form.[1]

De Quincey speaks to the same effect; quoting Wordsworth's remark that language or diction is "the incarnation of thought," not its dress, he goes on to say,

> In what proportion the thoughts are subjective, in that same proportion does the very essence become identical with the expression, and the style become confluent with the matter.[2]

In arriving at this conclusion, the English romantic critics were influenced by the Germans. Coleridge, in fact, had borrowed directly from A. W. Schlegel in formulating his definition of organic form.[3]

The followers of art for art's sake both in England and in France held the same view. Gautier put it thus:

> Nous n'avons jamais pu comprendre la séparation de l'idée et de la forme, pas plus que nous ne comprenons le corps

---

[1] "Shakespeare's Judgment Equal to His Genius," *Lectures on Shakespeare,* Works, IV, 55.

[2] Essays on Style, Part IV, Works (ed. D. Masson, London, 1890), X, 230.

[3] *Vorlesungen über dramatische Kunst und Litteratur,* Werke (Leipzig, 1846), VI, 157 (25th Vorlesung).

sans l'âme, ou l'âme sans le corps . . . une belle forme est une belle idée, car que serait-ce qu'une forme qui n'exprimerait rien? [1]

Flaubert's *Correspondance* is full of remarks expressing this conception. "Plus l'expression se rapproche de la pensée," he writes, "plus le mot colle dessus et dispairaît, plus c'est beau." [2] And again, "La forme sort du fond, comme la chaleur du feu." [3] Swinburne was speaking in both the English and the French tradition when he said that technical and spiritual beauty must be one: "If the handiwork be flawed, there must also have been some distortion or defect of spirit, a shortcoming or a misdirection of the spiritual supply." [4]

It is not surprising, then, that Pater shares the same idea. Sometimes he borrows the phrasing of Coleridge, praising Symons' poetry, for instance, for its "abundant poetic substance, developing as by its own organic force, the poetic forms proper to it." [5] A more characteristic expression of the idea is his praise of Coleridge's imaginative expression, "in which, in effect, the language itself is inseparable from, or essentially a part of, the thought." [6] He differs from the English tradition and allies himself to the French *l'art pour l'art*, not by the idea itself, but by the proportionate emphasis he gives to it.[7]

---

[1] *L'Artiste,* Dec. 1856.

[2] II, 71.

[3] II, 107.

[4] "Matthew Arnold's New Poems," Works, XV, 89.

[5] "A Poet With Something to Say," *Sketches and Reviews,* pp. 134–5.

[6] "Coleridge," *Appre.,* p. 93.

[7] A. J. Farmer has pointed out that De Quincey was a forerunner of Pater in his emphasis on the importance of form. See Farmer's *Walter Pater as a Critic of English Literature,* pp. 75–7.

The Aesthetic of Walter Pater

His doctrine of "the perfect identification of matter and form" [1] is the basis of his whole argument in *The School of Giorgione,* where he deduces from it that every artist must understand and abide by the limitations of the medium in which he is working.

> The sensuous material of each art brings with it a special phase or quality of beauty, untranslatable into the forms of any other. . . . Each art, therefore, having its own peculiar and untranslatable sensuous charm, has its own special mode of reaching the imagination, its own special responsibilities to its material.[2]

On that basis, too, he grounds his argument in the same essay that music is the highest of the arts, since it has in greatest degree the perfect fusion of form and content. This being true, all other arts are striving after the condition of music, that is, after complete identity of form and content, and are artistic in so far as they approach it. As a second corollary, it follows that lyric poetry is higher than poetry of "moral or political inspiration," "because in it we are least able to detach the matter from the form, without a deduction of something from that matter itself." [3] This second corollary is oddly at variance with the fact that Dante, Goethe, and Victor Hugo are the three writers to whom Pater refers most often and with greatest enthusiasm; and that in praising Hugo he speaks often of the novels, never of the poetry. His own uneasiness at finding himself on unsteady ground is perhaps indicated by his qualifying phrase: lyric poetry is the highest, "at least artistically."

[1] *Ren.,* p. 139. For a more recent and detailed exposition of the same idea, see A. C. Bradley, *Poetry for Poetry's Sake,* Oxford, 1901.
[2] *Ren.,* pp. 130–31.   [3] *Ibid.,* p. 137.

Formal Aspects of Art

It has been charged that there is in the long discussion in *The School of Giorgione* a tendency toward a confusion of the arts. This is true to a very limited extent, for Pater does concede in passing that each has an inclination toward the others, as "some of the most delightful music seems to be always approaching to figure, to pictorial definition," and architecture sometimes aims at fulfilling the conditions of sculpture, "as in the flawless unity of Giotto's tower at Florence."[1] But the whole purpose of the criticism is to insist on careful distinction. The long introduction is an argument that each artist must observe the limitations of his own medium. And the doctrine set forth there that all the arts constantly aspire toward the condition of music does not imply that they strive to become *like* music, but merely that they aspire to its *condition,* that is, perfect fusion of form and matter. Pater goes on at once to illustrate by showing that, in a picture, this perfect fusion is reached when the landscape depicted is thoroughly interpenetrated by the mood of the painter. The body of the essay then treats the school of Giorgione as an example of a school which understood the necessary limitations of the art of painting.

It is the same idea of the identity of form and content which is the basis of Pater's definition of style, found constantly throughout his work, and set forth especially in the essay called *Style.*

The term is right, and has its essential beauty, when it becomes, in a manner, what it signifies, as with the names of simple sensations. To give the phrase, the sentence, the structural member, the entire composition, song, or essay, a simi-

[1] *Ibid.,* p. 134.

lar unity with its subject and with itself:—style is in the right way when it tends towards that. All depends upon the original unity, the vital wholeness and identity, of the initiatory apprehension or view.[1]

This implies that form and matter must be completely fused in the creator's mind, quite apart from the material embodiment he is able to give them. It brings in its train the conclusion that the artist must then give perfect external shape, by words or colors or sounds, to the mental conception; in the completed work of art, the "extrinsication," as Croce would call it, must exactly embody the idea as he has conceived it. An earlier comment on Rossetti is significant.

> That he had this gift of transparency in language—the control of a style which did but obediently shift and shape itself to the mental motion, as a well-trained hand can follow on the tracing-paper the outline of an original drawing below it, was proved afterwards by a volume of typically perfect translations from the delightful but difficult 'early Italian poets': such transparency being indeed the secret of all genuine style, of all such style as can truly belong to one man and not to another.[2]

The principle of the absolute accordance of expression to idea is an "eclectic principle" which explains, justifies, and safeguards a variety of styles: "Scott's facility, Flaubert's deeply pondered evocation of 'the phrase,' " are equally artistic, because each writer has said what he willed to say, "in the simplest, most direct and exact manner possible." [3]

Although Pater was in both the romantic and the art for art's sake traditions in stressing the indivisible unity of form

[1] *Appre.*, p. 22.   [2] *Appre.*, pp. 206–7.   [3] "Style," *Appre.*, p. 34.

and content, it is clear that he was greatly influenced by Hegel in shaping his ideas. His first exposition on the subject of form was borrowed directly from Hegel, who had offered a classification of the arts based on their progress in two particulars: in the value of the spiritual content to be expressed; and in the degree to which the form was a perfect expression of the content.[1] This classification Pater reproduced in a very early essay, the *Winckelmann*.[2] In classic art, he says, the union of form and matter is complete, because the matter is such that it can be perfectly expressed in sensuous shape; it is an ideal art, "in which the thought does not outstrip or lie beyond the proper range of its sensible embodiment." The Venus of Melos "is in no sense a symbol, a suggestion, of anything beyond its own victorious fairness. The mind begins and ends with the finite image, yet loses no part of the spiritual motive." In contrast to the classic, oriental art displays an imperfect correspondence between the sensuous and the spiritual. "In the East from a vagueness, a want of definition, in thought, the matter presented to art is unmanageable." To put it in words not Pater's, the content is inadequate to the form. And again in the middle ages and modern times, the subject matter of art is equally unmanageable for its "exaggerated inwardness." The mind has come to boast its independence of the flesh, and to cherish thoughts and feelings too intangible and subjective to receive adequate external embodiment. It is now the form which is inadequate to the content. The different art forms correspond to these different steps in the mind's development. Architecture is best suited to express the vague spiritualities of the eastern world. Sculpture is pre-eminently

[1] Hegel, *Introduction*, ch. V. [2] *Ren.*, pp. 204–13, 230.

61

fitted to express the unchanging characteristics of man, in which the pagan world was interested. But painting, music, and poetry are the special arts of the more subjective medieval and modern world, because of their endless power of complexity. "Into these, with the utmost attenuation of detail, may be translated every delicacy of thought and feeling, incidental to a consciousness brooding with delight over itself."

So far, Pater has been following Hegel completely; but Hegel holds that modern life is turning to philosophy rather than art as the only possible mode of expressing our increasingly spiritual ideas. Pater, on the contrary, believes that the nineteenth-century arts of music and poetry, particularly the latter, are achieving a union of classicism and romanticism which makes them triumphant expressions of modern life. Goethe, for instance, "illustrates a union of the Romantic spirit, in its adventure, its variety, its profound subjectivity of soul, with Hellenism, in its transparency, its rationality, its desire of beauty." [1]

The Age of Athletic Prizemen, one of Pater's last essays, published in the year of his death, is based on the same Hegelian classification, treating Greek sculpture as expressive of a content which has not yet become too inward for perfect sensuous embodiment.

The essay on *The School of Giorgione,* published in 1877 and inserted in the third edition of the *Renaissance* in 1888, reveals further how much of Hegel Pater has made his own, and at what points he parts company with him. One of Hegel's main ideas was that art is the sensuous representation of the spiritual, addressing itself not merely to sensuous ap-

[1] *Ibid.,* pp. 226–7. See also pp. 230–1.

prehension nor to theoretic contemplation, but uniting in one indivisible unity the spiritual idea with the sensuous form.

> Inasmuch as the task of art is to represent the idea to direct perception in sensuous shape, and not in the form of thought or of pure spirituality as such, and seeing that this work of representation has its value and dignity in the correspondence and the unity of the two sides, i.e., of the Idea and its plastic embodiment, it follows that the level and excellency of art in attaining a realization adequate to its idea, must depend upon the grade of inwardness and unity with which Idea and Shape display themselves as fused into one.[1]

An idea must present itself in the first place to the mind of the artist, not as an abstract notion for which an external form must be sought, but as a concrete sensuous shape embodying the general in the individual from the very moment of mental birth.[2]

Pater puts exactly the same ideas briefly, though without any mention of Hegel: "art addresses not pure sense, still less the pure intellect, but the 'imaginative reason' through the senses." [3] In true art

> the constituent elements of the composition are so welded together, that the material or subject no longer strikes the intellect only; nor the form, the eye or the ear only; but form and matter, in their union or identity, present one single effect to the 'imaginative reason,' that complex faculty for

---

[1] *Intro.* (trs. Bosanquet), p. 174; see also pp. 102-14.

[2] *Ibid.*, pp. 110-11.

[3] *Ren.*, p. 130; see also *Plato and Platonism*, p. 140. The phrase 'imaginative reason' is used by Arnold; see for instance, "Pagan and Medieval Religious Sentiment," *Essays in Criticism*, 1st Series, Works (1903), III, 241. But Pater is giving it quite a different sense.

which every thought and feeling is twin-born with its sensible analogue or symbol.[1]

Of the two elements, spiritual and sensuous, Hegel stresses the spiritual as primary.

Art and its works as generated and created by the mind (spirit), are themselves of a spiritual nature, even if their mode of representation admits into itself the semblance of sensuous being, and pervades what is sensuous with mind . . . in works of art, mind has to do but with its own.[2]

Pater, with his greater interest in form, stresses the sensuous as fundamental.

In its primary aspect, a great picture has no more definite message for us than an accidental play of sunlight and shadow for a few moments on the wall or floor: is itself, in truth, a space of such fallen light, caught as the colours are in an Eastern carpet, but refined upon, and dealt with more subtly and exquisitely than by nature itself.[3]

But the sensuous is only the foundation for the rest.

This primary and essential condition fulfilled, we may trace the coming of poetry into painting, by fine gradations upwards; from Japanese fan-painting, for instance, where we get, first, only abstract colour; then, just a little interfused sense of the poetry of flowers; then, sometimes, perfect flower-painting; and so, onwards, until in Titian we have, as his poetry in the *Ariadne,* so actually a touch of true childlike humour in the diminutive, quaint figure with its silk gown, which ascends the temple stairs, in his picture of the *Presentation of the Virgin,* at Venice.[4]

[1] *Ren.,* p. 138.   [3] *Ren.,* p. 133.
[2] *Intro.,* p. 58.   [4] *Ibid.*

Formal Aspects of Art

When Pater argues in the same essay that music is the highest of the arts since it has in greatest degree the perfect fusion of form and content, he is choosing and rejecting from Hegel in accordance with his own emphasis on form. Hegel had held that music is the central of the modern arts, having the closest fusion between form and content; but he had considered poetry the highest, because most spiritual, and therefore most nearly adequate to express the infinitely complex and subjective spiritualities of the modern world; in it the content of consciousness becomes separated from the sensuous element and transcends it.[1] Pater, however, does not agree. In music, he says, "the end is not distinct from the means, the form from the matter, the subject from the expression; they inhere in and completely saturate each other. . . . In music, then, rather than in poetry, is to be found the true type or measure of perfected art."[2] This is far different from the reasoning of the German romantic poets such as Tieck, Novalis, and Wackenroder, who also put music at the peak of the arts. Infinite, eternal Being, the Germans thought, is constantly failing, being limited, petrified, and distorted by material embodiment. Music is the highest of the arts because it comes closest to expressing the inexpressible. It has a magical power of capturing the infinite.[3]

A second aspect of Pater's doctrine of form, more revolutionary from the English point of view, is his belief that while form and content are identical, form is the more impor-

[1] *Intro.*, pp. 207–9.
[2] *Ren.*, p. 139.
[3] See Wackenroder, "Das merkwürdige musikalische Leben des Tonkünstlers Joseph Berlinger," in *Phantasien über die Kunst*, ed. Tieck; and Novalis' *Schriften* (ed. Tieck and Schlegel, 1815), II, 142–7.

tant. These are not two contradictory ideas which he voices at different times, but are woven together constantly, put even into the same sentence. He speaks in one breath of "the mere matter" of a poem, and of the necessity of making form and matter indistinguishable.[1]

The notion that form must predominate over matter is not sanctioned by Hegel, nor is it in the main English tradition. It recalls rather the French school of *l'art pour l'art* whose members, in their passion for perfect workmanship, and in their exasperation with a public which seemed to have no appreciation of artistic perfection, frequently claimed that form was everything, matter of no importance at all. Gautier presented this in a metaphor.

> La forme, quoi qu'on ait dit, est tout. Jamais on n'a pensé qu'une carrière de pierre fût artiste de génie; l'important est la façon que l'on donne à cette pierre, car autrement, où serait la différence d'un bloc et d'une statue! . . . Le monde est la carrière, l'idée le bloc, et le poète le sculpteur.[2]

It was Flaubert who put the matter in most extreme fashion. In one of his letters he says that he would like to make a book about nothing at all, which should hold itself together by sheer force of style. "Les oeuvres les plus belles sont celles où il y a le moins de matière." [3] In their actual work, some of the French poets had a tendency to emphasize form at the expense of substance. Gautier tried to reproduce in his verses effects more directly obtained by painting and sculpture. Banville exercised the greatest virtuosity of verse technique in develop-

---

[1] "Giorgione," *Ren.,* p. 135.
[2] Gautier, *Victor Hugo* (Paris, Charpentier, 1902), sec. 18, pp. 103–4.
[3] *Correspondance,* II, 71.

ing comparatively trivial subjects. Baudelaire handled, not trivial subjects, but perverse and distorted ones, which gave the impression that he was depending purely on the artistic form to make them beautiful. He also cited with approval Poe's account of how the *Raven* was composed, working backward from the form to the thought and feeling rather than vice versa.[1]

Swinburne was echoing the ideas of the French when he said, "I . . . revere form or harmony as the high one law of all art." [2] He illustrated elsewhere by saying that if Dante, Shelley, and Hugo could have their moral sentiments stripped and reclothed in bad verse, the residue would be of no artistic importance; but that it might be possible to invert the sentiments, while retaining the manner and form, with no loss to art.[3]

The idea that form is more important than content was with these exponents of art for art's sake less a well developed aesthetic theory than an exaggeration to give a neglected element its proper importance. And yet they could have claimed a sober philosophic justification. Several German philosophers, beginning with Schiller, had worked out a systematic theory that form is *the* essential element in a work of art.[4] Schiller had taught that form is the essence, the spiritual shaping force, of an object, working from within outward; and there can be no true beauty till form has conquered matter.

[1] "La genèse d'un poëme," *Histoires extraordinaires,* Oeuvres, IX, 61-3.
[2] "Matthew Arnold's New Poems," Works, XV, 115.
[3] *Blake,* Works, XVI, 134.
[4] See R. F. Egan, "The Genesis of the Theory of 'Art for Art's Sake' in Germany and in England," for a detailed and penetrating study of this development.

The Aesthetic of Walter Pater

"In a really beautiful work of art, the substance ought to be inoperative, the form should do everything. . . . Consequently the true search of the master consists in *destroying matter by form.*"[1] Other German aestheticians of the period, such as Fichte and Schelling, differed in the details of their treatment, but agreed in emphasis: form is not merely a constituent element in art; it is *the* element which distinguishes a work of art from all other products of man's mind. Goethe, who had always believed that the work of art was shaped by the living spirit within, sometimes in his classical period followed Schiller in speaking of this shaping spirit as "form."[2] "The form alone ennobles the content," he said.[3]

In several places Pater seems to be expressing a similar conception. Montaigne he speaks of as "always on the lookout for the sincerities of human nature (sincerity counting for life-giving *form*, whatever the *matter* might be)."[4] Again he says:

That the mere matter of a poem, for instance, its subject, namely, its given incidents or situation—that the mere matter of a picture, the actual circumstances of an event, the actual topography of a landscape—should be nothing without the form, the spirit, of the handling, that this form, this mode of handling, should become an end in itself, should penetrate every part of the matter: this is what all art constantly strives after, and achieves in different degrees.[5]

In Plato's writings all the thoughts are old:

[1] *Über die ästhetische Erziehung des Menschen,* Briefe XXII, Werke (ed. Bellermann, Leipzig, 1895), VIII, 249.
[2] See for instance "Maximen und Reflexionen über Kunst," Werke, XXXV, 316–7.
[3] "Einzig veredelt die Form den Gehalt," *Pandora,* Werke, XV, 166.
[4] *Gaston,* p. 90.
[5] "Giorgione," *Ren.,* p. 135.

Formal Aspects of Art

Nothing but the life-giving principle of cohesion is new; the new perspective, the resultant complexion, the expressiveness which familiar thoughts attain by novel juxtaposition. In other words, the *form* is new. But then, in the creation of philosophical literature, as in all other products of art, *form*, in the full signification of that word, is everything, and the mere matter nothing.[1]

In analyzing Pater's remarks as to the superior importance of form, it is impossible to allocate influences. We are probably safe in saying that behind his own attitude there lay both a philosophic theory learned from the Germans and a desire like that of the French to impress the importance of artistic form on an unenlightened public.

In view of his other treatments of the subject, however, the concluding remarks of the essay on *Style* are rather surprising. There Pater makes a plea for the importance of "matter." The secret of art, he maintains as always, is the perfect identity of form and matter. This is "the condition of all artistic quality in things everywhere, of all good art." But it is not the primary test of *great* art, which depends for its greatness not on its form, but on its content. "It is on the quality of the matter it informs or controls, its compass, its variety, its alliance to great ends, or the depth of the note of revolt, or the largeness of hope in it, that the greatness of literary art depends, as *The Divine Comedy, Paradise Lost, Les Misérables, The English Bible*, are great art." Great art will have "something of the soul of humanity in it," and find "its logical, its architectural place, in the great structure of human life." [2] Here for once Pater abandons his usual attitude, in which he

---

[1] *Plato and Platonism*, p. 8.   [2] *Appre.*, p. 38. See *supra*, pp. 53–4.

thinks of spirit-given form as controlling mere brute matter, and adopts the more ordinary mode of thought, putting great subject matter as the prime requisite of great art.

It is interesting to speculate whether he may not have done this as a reaction to Flaubert's extreme position, for he had just read and reviewed the latter's *Correspondance,* and refers to him constantly throughout the essay. Flaubert, in his constant exaltation of form, had gone so far as to say, "Les oeuvres les plus belles sont celles où il y a le moins de matière." [1] Pater, in spite of his admiration for that great master of the *mot juste,* may have felt that he was going too far, and may have departed from his usual mode of speech in order to emphasize his own differing position.

2. THE CREATIVE PROCESS

Pater's most striking resemblance to the school of *l'art pour l'art* is his very similar attitude toward the process of artistic creation. The French group looked on the creative process as difficult and laborious; and they objected to the fluent fashion in which many of the romantics had written, apparently depending upon inspiration rather than on conscious artistry. Partly by theory and partly by temperament, they found writing a painful as well as a pleasurable process. Flaubert and the Goncourts went through a period of intense concentration which left them totally exhausted, as they endeavored to come to an adequate conception of a projected novel, living themselves into the lives of their characters. The difficulty of arriving at a satisfactory mental conception was naturally not as prolonged for the poets as for the novelists; but in both cases

[1] See *supra,* p. 66.

70

clothing the conception presented itself as a difficult task. Flaubert's search for 'the one word, the one phrase' has become famous. "J'ai été *cinq jours à faire une page* la semaine dernière," he says.[1] Gautier was the only one of the group to write easily, apparently at will. And yet he describes the life of an artist thus:

> Quelles luttes acharnées avec l'Idée, ce Protée insaisissable qui prend toutes les formes pour se dérober à votre étreinte, et qui ne rend son oracle que lorsqu'on l'a contrainte à se montrer sous son véritable aspect! Cette Idée, quand on la tient effarée et palpitante sous son genou vainqueur, il faut la relever, la vêtir, lui mettre cette robe de style si difficile à tisser, à teindre, à disposer en plis sévères ou gracieux. A ce jeu longtemps soutenu, les nerfs s'irritent, le cerveau s'enflamme, la sensibilité s'exacerbe; et la névrose arrive avec ses inquiétudes bizarres, ses insomnies hallucinées, ses souffrances indéfinissables.[2]

The style which these artists sought differed with the individual. The Goncourts aimed at a conversational effect, of which Flaubert disapproved. Flaubert strove for prose rhythm, euphony, beauty of effect. The poets sought for a lucid, rich, rather formal expression of their ideas. Aside from the Goncourts, the tendency was to approve a style which was the product of careful art. That is the purport of Gautier's poem on *L'art*:

> Oui, l'oeuvre sort plus belle
> D'une forme au travail
> Rebelle,
> Vers, marbre, onyx, émail.

. . . .

[1] *Correspondance,* II, 67.
[2] "Charles Baudelaire," *Portraits et souvenirs littéraires,* pp. 159–60.

The Aesthetic of Walter Pater

Sculpte, lime, cisèle;
Que ton rêve flottant
Se scelle
Dans le bloc résistant!

For all of them the service of beauty was no easy, light matter, but a high, difficult, austere devotion, calling for their very heart's blood.

In England the believers in art for art's sake were not united in any such devotion to the artistic conscience. Swinburne said nothing about the difficult, laborious search for the right word, for words came to him with almost fatal facility. Nor did he particularly admire the style which grew out of difficulties overcome. Of Blake's early verse he says, "Verse more nearly faultless and of a more difficult perfection was never accomplished. The sweet facility of being right, proper to great lyrical poets, was always an especial quality of Blake's." [1] In all his writing Swinburne assumes that perfection of form comes from a "sweet facility of being right," rather than from meticulous care. He feels that the creative process ought to be spontaneous, and objects to "marks of the chisel and the plane." [2] In this he is a long way from the French, and remains a part of the English romantic tradition; for the romantics saw creative activity as spontaneous and completely pleasurable; their theorists, Wordsworth and Coleridge, explained this pleasurable spontaneity by saying that the creative process implies the harmonious activity of all the writer's higher faculties in the act of imagination. Coleridge speaks of the poet as composing in that state "of pleasurable emotion,

[1] *Blake,* Works, XVI, 178.
[2] "Matthew Arnold's New Poems," Works, XV, 77.

which the exertion of all our faculties gives in a certain degree; but which can only be felt in perfection under the full play of those powers of mind, which are spontaneous rather than voluntary, and in which the effort required bears no proportion to the activity enjoyed." [1]

Pater's theory of the process of creation is a combination of the English romantic idea of spontaneous creation and of the French art for art's sake emphasis on laborious work. Apparently he feels that the mental conception comes with almost the flash of a happy inspiration, though it may be after a long period of waiting and thinking. The moment of artistic conception is the moment in which ideas, held only confusedly before, define themselves in the completely appropriate sensuous form. Leonardo waited with a perfect patience for "that moment of *bien-être,* which to imaginative men is a moment of invention," that happy moment in which, "the alchemy complete, the idea is stricken into colour and imagery." [2] Even with Flaubert, as Pater understood him, the mental act of creation was thus spontaneous, for Pater thinks that in every one of Flaubert's masterly sentences, "there was, below all mere contrivance, shaping and afterthought, by some happy instantaneous concourse of the various faculties of the mind with each other, the exact apprehension of what was *needed* to carry the meaning." [3]

But granted the initial conception in which the sensible analogue has been happily twin-born with the thought and feeling, there comes a period of long and patient labor, to transfer the mental conception to paper or canvas or marble.

[1] *Definition of Poetry,* Works, IV, 20.
[2] *Ren.,* pp. 113–4. [3] "Style," *Appre.,* p. 33.

Through many stages of refining, the artist attains clearness of expression. "He moves slowly over his work, calculating the tenderest tone, and restraining the subtlest curve, never letting hand or fancy move at large, gradually enforcing flaccid spaces to the higher degree of expressiveness." [1] This preoccupation of the writer with details of style is of course wholly in the service of the mental conception. Pater says that Flaubert labored with his writing, and boasted of his labor, because he knew that it set free "the innate lights of a true diamond"; it realized, and ministered to, his great imaginative gift.[2]

The emphasis on deliberate artistry, highly conscious form and polish, is present from the very beginning of Pater's work. In his early essay on Coleridge he criticized the latter's famous passage on organic unity in a highly significant fashion. Coleridge speaks of the organic form as innate, shaping as it develops itself from within.[3] Pater objected that this did not give sufficient credit to the infinitely careful workmanship of the artist.[4] As he developed, Pater's passion for studied, conscious artistry became even stronger. It found its first lengthy exposition in *Marius the Epicurean,* where the theory of Euphuism is presented through Flavian, who determined to make of literary expression a serious study, "weighing the precise power of every phrase and word, as though it were precious metal." [5] "This scrupulousness of literary art actually awoke in Flavian, for the first time, a sort of chivalrous conscience. What care for style! What patience of execution!

---

[1] "Coleridge," *Appre.,* p. 81.
[2] *Sketches and Reviews,* p. 78.
[3] See *supra,* p. 56.
[4] *Appre.,* pp. 80–1.
[5] I, 96.

What research for the significant tones of ancient idiom . . . !
What stately and regular word-building . . . !" [1] The whole
chapter on Euphuism is in praise of the "labor of the file."

Four years later the essay on *Style* offered a more lengthy
and more brilliant exposition of the same point of view. Pater
says that the literary artist will be a scholar, obeying the
"abundant and often recondite laws" of language, observing
its "limitations of vocabulary, structure, and the like." [2] "He
will feel the obligation not of the laws only, but of those
affinities, avoidances, those mere preferences, of his language,"
which have become established through literary usage. [3] He
will observe the most loving care in the handling of words,
restoring "the finer edge of words still in use," [4] and using
words compounded out of smaller particles with an awareness
of the latent metaphors in them. [5] And yet with all this care
for language, he will move freely within the prescribed limits.
In thoroughly mastering his instrument, he will be able to
manipulate it to his own use, thus attaining a completely original vocabulary and style.

The artist-scholar will especially strive to give his work
unity and structure.

> In literary as in all other art, structure is all-important, felt,
> or painfully missed, everywhere—that architectural concep-
> tion of work, which foresees the end in the beginning and
> never loses sight of it, and in every part is conscious of all
> the rest, till the last sentence does but, with undiminished
> vigour, unfold and justify the first. [6]

Restraint also is necessary for perfection. The artist-scholar

[1] I, 96-7.
[2] *Appre.*, p. 12.
[3] *Ibid.*, p. 13.
[4] *Ibid.*, p. 16.
[5] *Ibid.*, p. 20.
[6] *Ibid.*, p. 21.

will feel the pleasure of paring down his expression to the point of utmost fitness, for "self-restraint, a skilful economy of means, *ascêsis* . . . has a beauty of its own." [1] The whole matter of artistic fitness is a matter of getting rid of all but the indispensable.

> For in truth all art does but consist in the removal of surplusage, from the last finish of the gem-engraver blowing away the last particle of invisible dust, back to the earliest divination of the finished work to be, lying somewhere, according to Michelangelo's fancy, in the rough-hewn block of stone.[2]

In later writings, Pater praises particular men as artist-scholars: Professor Gosse, for instance, who is thoroughly familiar with the poetry of the past and works skilfully in its tradition; Pater feels that this scholarship does not raise him to the rank of a great poet, but it is much.[3] Plato, he says, wished to promote the art which demanded from the spectator a certain attentiveness; "and how satisfying, how reassuring, how flattering to himself after all, such work really is—the work which deals with one as a scholar, formed, mature and manly." [4] He even carries the same idea into other spheres of art. His essay on Raphael is an essay on the scholar-painter. The 'formula' which he finds to explain Raphael's genius is his willingness to learn from the other artists about him. The picture found in London, the Blenheim Madonna, shows him at the age of twenty-three, still definitely the scrupulous scholar, moving with the utmost care and restraint, with the jealous omissions dictated by good

[1] *Ibid.*, p. 17.
[2] *Ibid.*, pp. 19–20.
[3] *Guardian*, pp. 112–3.
[4] *Plato and Platonism*, p. 280.

taste. "He seems still to be saying, before all things, from first to last, 'I am utterly purposed that I will not offend.' " [1]

The praise of scholarship in art implies a preference for an elaborate, complex style, rather than a simple spontaneous one. Pater makes that preference explicit in the essay on *Style*: "One of the greatest pleasures of really good prose literature is the critical tracing out of that conscious artistic structure, and the pervading sense of it as we read." [2] He speaks again of "the delightful sense of difficulty overcome," [3] and, elsewhere, of "the charms of a patiently elaborated effect of art." [4] It is of course true that not all great art gives this effect of conscious elaboration, and he recognizes that fact. He admits that there is a "charm of ease," [5] and that there have been great writers who were directed by "unconscious tact" rather than deliberate art. The guiding principle of exact accordance of expression to idea explains and justifies all sorts of style, the most simple as well as the most complex.

But though he is careful to make allowances for a fluent or simple style, it is evident where his own preference lies. The essay on *Style* is in fact an explanation and a defense of his own particular mode of writing. Flaubert is used as its highest exemplar because of the obvious kinship between his workmanship and Pater's. Benson tells as that Pater was accustomed to jot down his main ideas on little slips of paper, then to write them out, leaving big spaces between the lines, which he later filled in with additions and fine qualifications. He would then copy the essay, again leaving spaces between

[1] *Misc. Studies*, p. 61.
[2] *Appre.*, pp. 24–5.
[3] *Ibid.*, p. 17.
[4] *Plato and Platonism*, p. 136.
[5] "Style," *Appre.*, p. 31.

the lines for another set of additions and qualifications. Sometimes he would even have the essay set up in type, so that he could see how it was going to look, and just where he needed to make further changes.[1] As he grew older his style gradually increased in complexity, becoming too involved and subtle for real strength. The *Renaissance* is not unusually difficult reading, but the later essays demand the closest attention if one is to grasp the main ideas, to say nothing of the fine nuances. That is one reason why the *Renaissance* is still his most popular book. But the later works have an especial appeal for "artist-scholars."

It might be expected that so strong an emphasis on form would vitiate Pater's criticism by arousing his admiration for works of art excellent in technique though lacking in substance. But he was saved from that error by his belief that form and content are identical, and by his own instinctive preference for the best. The unfortunate results of his over-emphasis are seen mainly in the excessive elaboration of his own later style, and in the exaggerations of his followers.

[1] *Walter Pater,* p. 202.

CHAPTER III

Life as an Art

I. BEING, NOT DOING; THE WEDDING OF EYE AND MIND

CERTAINLY THE MOST DISTINCTIVE element in Pater's aesthetic is his belief in life as an art. From the beginning he endeavored with almost religious earnestness to discover what principle would allow him to extract from life the last bit of value. All his strictly creative writings—the Conclusion to the *Renaissance, Marius the Epicurean, Gaston de Latour,* the *Imaginary Portraits, Emerald Uthwart,* and *The Child in the House*—are directed toward the problem of how to live. At the very threshold of his career he discovered the principle which he was to hold by till the end. With his usual delight in unifying apparently diverse ideas, he shaped a theory of life to conform with his theory of art. Life, he said, should be lived in the spirit of art. And as art was to be enjoyed for its own sake, so life also was to be lived for its own sake, not as a means to some far goal, but as an end in itself.

The first essay which we have preserved for us, *Diaphaneitè,* written to be read before his friends of the Old Mortality at Oxford, is a description of the artistic character. As in art the form is a perfect expression of the content, so in an artistic life the outward activity is a perfect expression of the inward soul. The ideal character is transparent, letting into the inner nature all that is valuable in the external order, and allowing the inner soul to show transparently in the outward act.[1]

Even as early as this first essay, life as an end in itself meant for Pater a life of contemplation and feeling, rather than of action. In *Diaphaneitè* he expresses this unfortunately. The "diaphanous" character has such a perfect equipoise of gifts, virtues, and interests that it can follow no single bent, and therefore can take no active part in life. It has "a moral sexlessness, a kind of impotence, an ineffectual wholeness of nature, yet with a divine beauty and significance of its own." [2] And still such colorless characters are of ultimate value; they "fill up the blanks between contrasted types of character," and are a "delicate provision in the organization of the moral world for the transmission to every part of it of the life quickened at single points." [3] And so the "diaphanous" soul is better fitted to be the "basement type" than the philosopher, the saint, the artist, or the pedant, for "a majority of such would be the regeneration of the world." [4]

Pater's next elaboration of the subject, far more convincing, came in the essay on Wordsworth. Here he speaks of the majority of mankind, hurrying always to some definite end; "but the end may never be attained, and the means not be quite the right means."

Meantime, to higher or lower ends, they move too often with something of a sad countenance, with hurried and ignoble gait, becoming, unconsciously, something like thorns, in their anxiety to bear grapes.

[1] *Passim, Misc. Studies.*
[2] *Ibid.,* p. 253.
[3] *Ibid.,* p. 248.
[4] *Ibid.,* p. 254.

And so they become spiritually thin and impoverished, "thus diminishing the sum of perfection in the world at its very sources." [1] Instead of picturing all things in life under the figure of machinery, simply means to an end, we should take for our aim "impassioned contemplation," *"being,* rather than *doing,"* and try to develop "those *manners* which are, in the deepest as in the simplest sense, *morals,* and without which one cannot so much as offer a cup of water to a poor man without offence." [2] Pater considers Wordsworth one of the great teachers of this ideal.[3] Note that in speaking of machinery, he is borrowing a figure of speech from Arnold.[4] But Arnold's point is that we should not value as ends in themselves what are actually mere machinery to an end—such things as large population, great wealth, an impressive church organization,—the true end being character. Pater's point is quite different—that we should pass over nothing whatever as mere machinery, but should so handle everything we are concerned with as to give to it or find in it a value in itself. But for him also the end is character.

Pater's most lengthy treatment of life lived in the spirit of art is found in *Marius the Epicurean,* where he shows Marius

[1] *Appre.,* p. 60.

[2] *Ibid.,* p. 61.

[3] *Ibid.,* pp. 59–63. Cf. Wordsworth's own remark about "the inherent superiority of contemplation to action . . . as proceeding and governing all action that moves to salutary purposes; and, secondly, as leading to elevation, the absolute possession of the individual mind, and to a consistency or harmony of the being within itself, which no outward agency can reach to disturb or to impair; and lastly, as producing works of pure science; or of the combined faculties of imagination, feeling, and reason; works which . . . are entitled rightly to take place of the noblest and most beneficent deeds of heroes, statesmen, legislators, or warriors." "Letter to the Editor of the *Friend,"* Prose Works, I, 99–100.

[4] "Sweetness and Light," *Culture and Anarchy,* Works, VI, 14–40.

adopting the principle of "Life as the end of Life," [1] and pondering on how one can best "live days 'lovely and pleasant' in themselves, here and now." [2] In his last book, *Plato and Platonism*, he is still touching on the same problem, this time presenting the artistic life under the figure of music.[3]

Another constant element in Pater's aesthetic of life is his insistence on the wedding of eye and mind, the union of the visible and the invisible. This springs from his own physical and mental constitution, and furnishes the temperamental basis for his philosophy of the identity of artistic form and content. One of his first essays protests against Coleridge's forgetting the world of form and color in the search for abstract ideas,[4] and another praises Winckelmann for his native tendency to "escape from abstract theory to intuition, to the exercise of sight and touch." [5] The account of Florean Deleal, the 'Child in the House,' is an illuminating description of Pater himself.

> In later years he came upon philosophies which occupied him much in the estimate of the proportion of the sensuous and the ideal elements in human knowledge, the relative parts they bear in it; and, in his intellectual scheme, was led to assign very little to the abstract thought, and much to its sensible vehicle or occasion. Such metaphysical speculation did but reinforce what was instinctive in his way of receiving the world, and for him, everywhere, that sensible vehicle or occasion became, perhaps only too surely, the necessary concomitant of any perception of things, real enough to be of any weight or reckoning, in his house of thought.[6]

[1] I, 143.
[2] I, 148. See I, chs. 8, 9, *passim*.
[3] See chs. 3, 8, especially pp. 70, 200, 206.

[4] *Appre.*, p. 68.
[5] *Ren.*, p. 184.
[6] *Misc. Studies*, p. 186

Life as an Art

Such passages as this would seem to imply concern for the visible with little regard for the invisible embodied therein. But this is never Pater's real meaning, as a reading of the context will always show. He is concerned with form as it expresses soul.

The inability to separate the invisible from the visible accounts for the method adopted in *Marius the Epicurean*. Each philosophy of life—the Epicurean, the Stoic, the Christian—comes to Marius embodied in a personality. What Pater said later of Plato was true of himself and of his other self, Marius; the eyes of both were on "*character* as seen in *characteristics*";[1] for them both, "all knowledge was like knowing a *person*";[2] they had, like Plato, a "sensuous love of the unseen."[3]

Allied to this demand for the visible embodiment of the invisible spirit is Pater's persistent refusal to credit any reality which cannot be proved. He rejects any transcendental reality, in whatever form presented.[4] Even in his later days, when he evidently yearned to believe the Christian doctrine, he insisted on keeping an open mind on whatever cannot be proved.[5] The values which he accepts are only those which he believes to have the backing of experience. *Marius* shows clearly his belief in the necessity of "verification"; Marius values only "facts," discoverable by experience. Cyrenaicism seems to him plausible, because it has "no basis of unverified

---

[1] *Plato and Platonism,* p. 130.

[2] *Ibid.,* p. 129.

[3] *Ibid.,* p. 143. See ch. 6 *passim.*

[4] See "Coleridge," *Appre., passim,* and *Plato and Platonism,* pp. 40–50, 195.

[5] See *infra,* pp. 95–6.

hypothesis," [1] whereas the complete theory of Heraclitus is "hypothesis only—the hypothesis he actually preferred, as in itself most credible, . . . yet still . . . but one unverified hypothesis, among many others." [2] Marius has always feared Stoicism, as it seemed to demand the admission of first principles which might "distort the revelations of the experience of life"; [3] but in listening to the Stoic orator he realizes that he has been ignoring a large proportion of "the facts of life"; [4] and he inquires, in regard to the Stoic commonwealth of which Fronto speaks, "where was that comely order, to which as a great fact of experience he might give its due?" [5] He is led on to Christianity by the inquiry, "Were there . . . beliefs, without which life itself must be almost impossible, principles which had their sufficient ground of evidence in that very fact?" [6] Pater's need for the visible, palpable, makes him an empiricist.

2. GROWING EMPHASIS ON UNIVERSAL ORDER AND ON LIVING IN THE IDEAL

Across these constant strands in Pater's theory of life as an art there plays another set of ideas, changing and developing gradually. These concern themselves with the constitution of the universe and the best means of adapting oneself to it.

We may judge Pater's early self not only by his writing through the *Renaissance,* but also by his account of the youthful ideas of the 'Child in the House,' and of Marius the

[1] I, 149.
[2] I, 132.
[3] II, 6.
[4] II, 9.
[5] II, 12.
[6] II, 64.

Epicurean, whose soul-histories are obviously in the main Pater's own. Putting together these sources of information, we discover that Pater in his young manhood was much impressed by the bewildering whirl of universal change. "What is secure in our existence is but the sharp apex of the present moment between two hypothetical eternities, and all that is real in our experience but a series of fleeting impressions." [1] This is the old Heraclitean doctrine of flux, which finds a famous expression in the Conclusion to the *Renaissance*. Matter is but a combination of elements which are constantly shifting, and "birth and gesture and death and the springing of violets from the grave are but a few out of ten thousand resultant combinations." [2] Our own physical life is but a perpetual motion of these elements, and our inward life of feeling and thought shows a still more rapid whirlpool, a still more eager and devouring flame. If we scrutinize ourselves, we find in the last analysis, a "continual vanishing away," a "strange, perpetual weaving and unweaving of ourselves." [3]

To be sure, this constant change proceeds according to law. Pater belongs to the late nineteenth century and could hardly have escaped the nineteenth-century belief in evolution. Modern science, he says, reveals to us "types of life evanescing into each other by inexpressible refinements of change." [4] But though from the first he recognized this element of law, [5] he felt that unfortunately the change was much more in evidence than the order. Man must cultivate the qualities necessary to

[1] *Marius*, I, 146.
[2] P. 234.
[3] *Ibid.*, p. 236.
[4] "Coleridge," *Appre.*, p. 66.
[5] *Ibid.*, pp. 65–8.

cope with a universe disturbingly in flux about and within him.[1]

There are two ways to meet the flux of life:—one must be sensitive, to make the most of it; and one must be stable, to resist it. In a formal aesthetic, these two methods would correspond to the two main characteristics of art, richness of content and unity of form.

The first response, sensitivity, is the one about which we hear most in discussions of Pater. It is described in the Conclusion to the *Renaissance,* and later explained at length in *Marius.* One should cultivate and refine the perceptive powers of the mind—the powers of sense perception, of emotion, and of intellect—till one's whole nature becomes a single complex medium of reception.[2] One is thus enabled to feel a "quickened sense of life," a "quickened, multiplied consciousness," to be "present always at the focus where the greatest number of vital forces unite in their purest energy." Success in life is "to maintain this ecstasy."[3] This seems a natural outgrowth of romanticism, of the Keatsian longing for a "Life of Sensations rather than of Thoughts"—that is, for a life of vivid emotionalized apprehensions, rather than of truths reached through reason.[4] We are not to judge the worth of these pulsations of

[1] There is a decided similarity between these presuppositions, and the views of Herbert Spencer. Spencer stresses the constant and complicated change of matter from form to form, following the law of evolution. (See *First Principles* [1862], part II, especially chs. 8, 9, 12, 13.)

[2] *Marius,* I, 147.

[3] "Conclusion," *Ren.,* pp. 236–9.

[4] Letter to Bailey, 22nd November, 1817, *Letters* (ed. M. Buxton Forman, Oxford, 1931), I, 68. Cf. also Wordsworth's ideal of high sensibility as expressed in the Preface to the *Lyrical Ballads,* and Hazlitt's demand for "common sense"—that is, apprehension through living ("Common Sense and Genius," *Table Talk,* Works, VIII, 31–50).

intense consciousness merely by their immediate strength, Pater comes to emphasize in his mature period. We are to judge them primarily from the way they will appear to memory, and the value the soul will set on them in looking backward.[1] Neither are we to cultivate any and every intense experience for the sake of its intensity. We must select the valuable. Education should teach us to recognize the ideal elements of everyday life and to live exclusively in them.[2]

The relativity of phenomena, though a fundamentally pessimistic doctrine, will bring its advantages. The very fact that phenomena are so evanescent, combinations so fleeting, and nuances so delicate, stimulates us to finer and finer discriminations; we become absorbed in distinguishing delicate detail.[3] Goethe is the best example of this speculative temper, for he is one "to whom every moment of life brought its contribution of experimental, individual knowledge; by whom no touch of the world of form, colour, and passion was disregarded."[4] Further, appreciation of the relativity of all things begets not only an intellectual *finesse* but a "delicate and tender justice in the criticism of human life." It gives elasticity to inflexible principles, and enables us to judge more sympathetically and truly.[5]

But while we must be sensitive, to gain the most from every moment as it passes, we must encompass the equally difficult task of achieving a sense of stability and permanence in spite of the constant change. The two early essays on *Diaphaneitè* and *Winckelmann*, the *Greek Studies, Marius the Epicurean,*

---

[1] *Marius,* I, 45, 154.
[2] *Ibid.,* 53–4.
[3] "Coleridge," *Appre.,* p. 67.
[4] *Ibid.,* p. 68.
[5] *Ibid.,* p. 103.

and the lectures on *Plato and Platonism* all deal with this problem.

In the essay on Winckelmann, Pater finds the eternal problem of culture to be "balance, unity with one's self, consummate Greek modelling."[1] This is the lesson which the young Goethe learned from Winckelmann,—the necessity of wholeness, unity, integrity. Of course, in the modern world, with its tangled interests and its conflicting claims, "unity with ourselves, in blitheness and repose," is far harder to achieve than it was for the Greeks, but it is just as important as ever. It can no longer be achieved by joyful union with the external world, nor by the development of any single talent. It must be attained as Goethe attained it, by "a watchful exigent intellectualism."[2] Winckelmann is the example of a man who attained unity, sacrificing every other interest to his one supreme enthusiasm, art. Goethe's unity is of a higher type than that of Winckelmann, because he tested all the various forms of culture one after another—such as absorption in the sensuous, preoccupation with metaphysics, the other-worldliness of the *Schöne Seele*—and by this means discovered and developed his own strength.[3] The complete, well-rounded culture so attained he expressed in the practical form of art production.[4]

One may judge from Pater's references that Goethe played a large part in developing in him an admiration for these two

---

[1] *Ren.,* p. 228.

[2] *Ibid.*

[3] This is presumably what Pater meant when he said, à propos of Da Vinci, "The way to perfection is through a series of disgusts." ("Leonardo," *Ren.,* p. 103.) But the latter expression is easy to misinterpret.

[4] *Ren.,* pp. 228–30.

ways of meeting life—extreme receptiveness to all that is valuable in the flux, and a stability and unity which resist the disintegrating power of the universe in motion around one. He quotes Goethe several times in favor of the latter, and uses him as the best example of each.

In his early work Pater did not bring the two methods specifically together. But as he grew older, he became increasingly impressed with the necessity of a balance between them. This is first expressed in the *Marbles of Aegina,* in 1880, where he finds in Greek art and life two tendencies: "There is the centrifugal, the Ionian, the Asiatic tendency, flying from the centre, working with little forethought straight before it, in the development of every thought and fancy; . . . delighting in brightness and colour, in beautiful material, in changeful form everywhere." [1] The other is the Doric or "salutary European tendency, which, finding human mind the most absolutely real and precious thing in the world, enforces everywhere the impress of its sanity, its profound reflexions upon things as they really are, its sense of proportion." [2] Both aspects of man's soul are equally important, and must be held in balance. Pater had twice earlier referred to the centrifugal or Asiatic force in opposition to the centripetal or Doric,[3] but without any stress on the need for poise between them. In his last book he recurs to them again, saying that the Greek state

[1] *Greek Studies,* p. 252.

[2] *Ibid.,* p. 253. In discussing the centrifugal and centripetal tendencies Pater borrows from Nietzsche, when he identifies the one with the worship of Dionysus and the other with the worship of Apollo. But he does not use the terms 'Dionysian' and 'Apollonian' in Nietzsche's sense. See Nietzsche's *Birth of Tragedy* (1870–1), Works (trs. Wm. A. Haussmann, London, 1909), I, *passim,* but especially pp. 21–43.

[3] "Coleridge's Writings," *Westminster Rev.* (Jan. 1866), LXXXV, 113 (*Appre.,* p. 71) ; and "Demeter and Persephone," *Greek Studies,* p. 119.

finally went to pieces because the Asiatic centrifugal forces were not properly balanced by the Doric centripetal.[1]

As Pater grew older, he came to feel less keenly the flux of life. He had always been impressed with the order of the human reason. Now he came to feel more keenly the order pervading the universe. In *Marius the Epicurean* he wonders whether there may not be a divine plan behind it all, and is half convinced. He has Marcus Aurelius say, "Could there be *Cosmos,* that wonderful, reasonable order, in him, and nothing but disorder in the world without?" [2] His last book, *Plato and Platonism,* is full of recognitions of a universal order. He praises Pythagorus, for instance, who fulfilled the true purpose of philosophy, "to realize unity in variety, to discover *cosmos*—an order that shall satisfy one's reasonable soul—below and within apparent chaos." [3]

Along with this emphasis on order goes a stress on external discipline, as a means of producing order within the soul. One of the central ideas of *Emerald Uthwart* is the discipline and correction which Emerald received from his experiences at the King's School, Canterbury. In *Plato and Platonism* Pater speaks again of that fitness "which it is the business of the fine arts to convey into material things, of the art of discipline to enforce upon the lives of men"; [4] and he devotes a whole chapter to the *ascêsis* which Plato considered a feature of the education of the Lacedaemonian youth.

The growing emphasis on order and discipline is, however, only part of a larger development of Pater's outlook on life, a development which included his attitude toward religion and

[1] *Plato and Platonism,* pp. 22–5.
[2] II, 39.
[3] P. 52.
[4] P. 36.

Life as an Art

morals, as well as his whole philosophy of the universe. Since he has given us the story in detail, with a thin fictitious disguise, in *Marius the Epicurean,* we may well follow it there, for the light which it throws on the ideals which Pater must have absorbed in his own boyhood, the effect on his philosophy of a first contact with a more sophisticated world, and the forces which finally drew him strongly toward the Christian religion.

When Marius was a child, he had been devoutly brought up in the old Roman country religion, with its pious observances centering in the home, "a religion of usages and sentiment rather than of facts and beliefs." His own innate religious sense responded strongly to this piety, and felt with quiet reverence the presence of "conscious powers external to ourselves, pleased or displeased by the right or wrong conduct of every circumstance of daily life." Expecting to be a priest, he acquired a love of order, a "sort of mystic enjoyment" in "the abstinence, the strenuous self-control and *ascêsis*" which even the first stages of preparation for that sacred function involved. After he had abandoned this intention, it still left him an aspiration toward "a sort of hieratic beauty and order in the conduct of life." He acquired also, in these early days, a sympathy for the sufferings of all creatures, especially the animals, a reverence for the body as handmaid of the soul, and a passionate love of visible beauty.[1]

This account cannot be taken as a literal narrative of Pater's own boyhood. But it has nevertheless a core of truth. We know from his biographers that he looked forward to taking orders in the Church of England, and from the *Child in the*

[1] I, chs. 1–3.

91

House that three of the strongest forces in his childhood were his religious sense, his pity for suffering, and his love of beautiful form.

When Marius left home, after the death of his mother, and went to school in Pisa, he came in contact with an exciting new world. Becoming a sceptic, he embraced the natural doctrine of brilliant youth, "unlimited self-expansion in a world of various sunshine," which he saw partially embodied in his gifted friend Flavian. In reasoning out his new outlook, Marius pondered over the beliefs of Heraclitus, who recognized the constant, ceaseless flux of all the elements, and at the same time saw back of that perpetual flux "a continuance . . . of orderly intelligent relationships . . . ordinances of the divine reason, maintained throughout the changes of the phenomenal world." But like the Cyrenaics, Marius was more impressed by the change, which he could see for himself, than by the Divine Plan back of it, which was purely hypothetical. He developed "a scepticism almost dryly practical," which emphasized the possibility that if an outward world really does exist, we may not apprehend it truly. Since, therefore, one can never know the world as it really is, all one can do is to make sure of his own impressions and live in them, to cultivate all his receptive powers, and "to yield himself to the improvement of the present with an absolutely disengaged mind." The practical ideal to which this pointed was not mere pleasure, but "a general completeness of life," "a life of various yet select sensations," an intense appreciation of all the beautiful things in the world—nature, human passions, particularly art.[1]

[1] I, chs. 4–9, especially chs. 8, 9.

Life as an Art

Here again, though we are not to suppose that Pater actually had a friend like Flavian, and sat down in his young manhood to ponder upon Heraclitus, we recognize the frame of mind which produced the Conclusion to the *Renaissance,* with its emphasis on constant change, on the impossibility of ever knowing the world as it really is, and on the need for sharpening our perceptive faculties to seize the best from out its ceaseless whirl.

The attitude of Marius in this Cyrenaic period toward the problem of morality is interesting. He himself practiced the essence of morality—kindness toward others—from mingled impulses of natural affection, enlightened self-interest, fear of penalties, and mere conformity to attractive custom.[1] But he reflected thus:

> It was intelligible that this "aesthetic" philosophy might find itself (theoretically, at least, and by way of a curious question in casuistry, legitimate from its own point of view) weighing the claims of that eager, concentrated, impassioned realization of experience, against those of the received morality. Conceiving its own function in a somewhat desperate temper, and becoming, as every high-strung form of sentiment, as the religious sentiment itself, may become, somewhat antinomian, when, in its effort towards the order of experiences it prefers, it is confronted with the traditional and popular morality, at points where that morality may look very like a convention, or a mere stage property of the world, it would be found, from time to time, breaking beyond the limits of the actual moral order; perhaps not without some pleasurable excitement in so bold a venture.[2]

He admitted to himself that this challenge to the received

[1] II, 7.   [2] I, 149-50.

morality might be dangerous for some weak souls, but insisted that it was not to be taken as a discarding of real moral values:

> Not pleasure, but fulness of life, and "insight" as conducting to that fulness—energy, variety, and choice of experience, including noble pain and sorrow even, loves such as those in the exquisite old story of Apuleius, sincere and strenuous forms of the moral life, such as Seneca and Epictetus—whatever form of human life, in short, might be heroic, impassioned, ideal: from these the "new Cyrenaicism" of Marius took its criterion of values.[1]

Whether Pater himself went through any such process of reasoning in his youth, we do not know. The only indication we have of it is the one statement in the Conclusion to the *Renaissance*:

> The theory or idea or system which requires of us the sacrifice of any part of this [our own] experience, in consideration of some interest into which we cannot enter, or some abstract theory we have not identified with ourselves, or of what is only conventional, has no real claim upon us.[2]

His own life seems always to have been pure and ascetic. Possibly he was not so much tracing in *Marius* his own earlier reasoning on this point, as he was reading a lesson to those so-called disciples of his who had practiced a morality so much less austere than his own.

The rest of the two volumes of *Marius* is particularly interesting to us because it shows what Pater came to consider lacking in this early philosophy, and what values he set highest. When Marius went to Rome, ambitious to be a writer, and

[1] I, 151–2. [2] Pp. 237–8.

Life as an Art

became amanuensis to the Stoic Emperor Marcus Aurelius, his gradually maturing mind realized that his earlier doctrine was not complete. Pretending to a pragmatic sanction, that of making the most out of life, it actually fell short in many particulars. It offered no criterion for distinguishing between values in life—if it had not been for the moral values which Marius had brought with him from his early religious upbringing, he might have made many wrong choices.[1] With its philosophy of continuous change it offered nothing permanent for the soul to hold by.[2] It did not do away with fear, either "the terror of mere bodily evil," or the dread of death.[3] And in its insistence on relying only on one's own individual experience, it did not take into account the larger humanity of which the individual is inevitably a part; it shut out, that is, the "old morality," which rests on the experiences of the best men over the long history of the world. Presently Marius was persuaded by a speech of the Stoic orator, Fronto, to believe that a right regard for the larger wisdom and experience of mankind demanded an acceptance of the established morality.[4]

Other Stoic ideas which he saw embodied in the Emperor Marcus Aurelius attracted him greatly, particularly the belief in a Pervading Reason which "sweetly ordereth all things." Aurelius, to be sure, recognized that this is a hypothesis rather than a certainty; that man is really in a dilemma to know whether to believe in Chance or Divine Wisdom. But the Stoic theory says that one can control one's thoughts, and choose to believe whatever seems the highest; he therefore deliberately

[1] II, 107.
[2] II, 18.
[3] I, 166.
[4] II, chs. 15, 16, *passim.*

95

chose to believe in Order. Marius was much impressed with this theory of the will as vision, as a way of arriving at truth. But his own temperament, so wedded to the actual, the palpable, would not allow him to make use of it himself.[1]

During the time of his contact with the Stoic Emperor, Marius also gradually became acquainted with the Christian soldier, Cornelius. Yearning for a more satisfactory basis of life than his youthful Cyrenaicism, he constantly compared the two men and their doctrines, and was drawn always more strongly toward Christianity. From the beginning Cornelius seemed to him the embodiment of joy and hope, whereas Aurelius, with his acceptance of the world as it is, had a suppressed melancholy. And when Marius came to know Christianity, he recognized hope as one of its central aspects,—the hope of a future life, of the conquest of this world's evil. The "Good Shepherd, serene, blithe and debonair," the king of peace among men, represents "the final consummation of that bold and brilliant hopefulness in man's nature, which had sustained him so far through his immense labours, his immense sorrows, and of which pagan gaiety in the handling of life, is but a minor achievement." [2]

Even more important than the joyfulness of Christianity was the kindness and pity which it enjoined. Before Marius had pondered on Christianity at all, he had revolted against the cruelty that made possible the scenes of the amphitheatre. He now contrasted Marcus Aurelius and Cornelius: Aurelius who could sit indifferently through those scenes of cruelty, because he accepted in passive resignation the evil and suffering in the world, and met it with the doctrine that pain does

[1] II, ch. 19. Cf. also II, 90, 91.   [2] II, chs. 21 (2), 22.

not exist if one does not admit it; and Cornelius, who recognized all evil as definitely evil, "an enemy with whom no terms could be made, visible, hatefully visible, in a thousand forms." But even above the suffering which it is in man's power to fight, Marius saw an unkindness in the nature of things which no charity or determination on the part of man can get at— inevitable pain, old age, death. What is needed to make such evil bearable is "a certain permanent and general power of compassion" in the world. Christianity, as a matter of course, supplied active charity, and where that could not help, a tender sympathy.[1]

Almost as important with Marius as its pity was the humanism of Christianity. In the period of the Antonines, when the church was feeling no persecution, it developed, not a one-sided, narrow, austere Puritanism, but a large, generous acceptance of all sides of life. Marius had objected to the Stoic theory because in its milder forms it taught a "gentle contempt" for all the material aspects of life, and in the form which Aurelius held, an actual contempt for the things of the body. In contrast, "the very person of Cornelius was nothing less than a sanction of that reverent delight Marius had always had in the visible body of man." The Christian reverence for all things made for the highest type of life. All the various affections of family life were developed "into large controlling passions"; chastity, in the broadest sense, was inspired, and so was cheerful industry, "peaceful labour, after the mind, the

---

[1] I, ch. 14; II, chs. 18, 25. Miss Young points out that the concept of sympathy is a widespread philosophic concept of Pater's day, adopted by positivists to account for those social instincts of man which seemed not sufficiently accounted for on utilitarian principles. *The Writings of Walter Pater*, pp. 47–8, 67, 92–6.

pattern, of the workman of Galilee." The Christian life was beautiful, with a beauty of outward things as well as of inward. One manifestation of this spirit was the nobly beautiful liturgy, which satisfied "the natural soul of worship" in Marius as it had never been satisfied before.[1]

The central doctrine of Christianity which Marius longed to believe is the doctrine of a Divine Creator behind all things, actually a companion and friend to man.[2] He had had a foretaste of that doctrine when he had recognized the self-communings of Marcus Aurelius as really a communion with the divine reason in man, and had realized his own longing for such companionship. He had even felt for a few uplifted hours the consoling sense of it. In his short life that sense never came again, but it "gave him a definitely ascertained measure of his moral or intellectual need." As he lay dying, soon after, he drew comfort for his lack of faith by reflecting that he had always kept himself ready to receive experience and to enlarge his soul by it; now, as he was facing death, his soul was still unclouded, and receptive to fresh truth. At last he would know![3]

It has been said that the magnet which drew Pater to Christianity was purely aesthetic, the beauty of holiness. This is true, as the foregoing summary shows, only if we expand the meaning of the word 'beauty' to its largest scope, and make it include much more than the charm of the church ritual. Evidently the strongest forces in the older Pater were a feeling of sympathy with mankind, which showed itself in tenderness for all suffering, and in an acceptance, intellectual as well as

[1] II, 53–4; chs. 21 (2)–23.   [3] II, chs. 19, 28.
[2] II, 47–51, 66–72, 184–5, 218.

98

practical, of the moral system evolved through the experience of the race; a desire for a gracious, many-sided life, developing the body, the senses, the intellect, the passions, the will; and an unsatisfied longing for belief in a Divine Companion.

In Pater's work after *Marius* there are many implications which support the information we have gained from that book and help to define his mature attitude toward religious faith. What he expects of religion is indicated in his remark about Plato, who seems to "promise all, or almost all, that in a later age natures great and high have certainly found in the Christian religion." For Plato, that is, philosophy is

> nothing less than an "escape from the evils of the world," and ὁμοίωσις τῷ Θεῷ, a being made like to God. It provides a satisfaction not for the intelligence only but for the whole nature of man, his imagination and faith, his affections, his capacity for religious devotion, and for some still unimagined development of the capacities of sense.[1]

A number of times in his later work Pater recurred to the idea that each man's beliefs are dependent on his temperament.[2] And a number of times he indicated that his own temperament disposed him to scepticism of what cannot be seen or proved. There are two divergent influences, he says, coming from Plato's work: the belief in the Absolute; and the sceptical temper, fostered by his dialectic method, the never-ceasing, never-satisfied search for truth. Of these two influences, we of the modern age inevitably submit to the

[1] *Plato and Platonism,* p. 264.
[2] "Van Storck," *Imag. Por.,* especially pp. 107–8, 112; "Browne," *Appre.,* pp. 159–60.

latter, even though we live our lives in the spirit of the former.

> There they stand, the two great landmarks of the intellectual or spiritual life as Plato conceived it: the ideal, the world of "ideas," "the great perhaps," for which it is his merit so effectively to have opened room in the mental scheme, to be known by us, if at all, through our affinities of nature with it, which, however, in our dealings with ourselves and others we may assume to be objective or real:—and then, over against our imperfect realization of that ideal, in ourselves, in nature and history, amid the personal caprices (it might almost seem) of its discovery of itself to us, as the appropriate attitude on our part, the dialectical spirit, which to the last will have its diffidence and reserve, its scruples and second thoughts. Such condition of suspended judgment indeed, in its more genial development and under felicitous culture, is but the expectation, the receptivity, of the faithful scholar, determined not to foreclose what is still a question—the "philosophic temper," in short, for which a survival of query will be still the salt of truth, even in the most absolutely ascertained knowledge.[1]

But though we must always be sceptical, because we cannot prove the existence of the One, we must never close our minds to the possibility that the unprovable may nevertheless be true: "Bring . . . the Great Possibility at least within the lines of your plan—your plan of action or production; of morality; especially of your conceptions of religion." [2] As his biographers tell us, Pater was a faithful, devout attendant at the church services. He is one of those people he himself describes, who "make allowance in their scheme of life for a

[1] *Plato and Platonism,* pp. 195–6.
[2] "Amiel's 'Journal Intime,' " *Guardian,* p. 35.

Life as an Art

great possibility, and with some of them that bare concession of possibility (the subject of it being what it is) becomes the most important fact in the world." [1]

There is another development in Pater's thought which can be more briefly traced, since it is only a different side of a development which has already been set forth at length, that is, his increasing emphasis on the ideal. As we might expect, his changing view of life proves to be at the root of that growing conception of art. In his early work he does not discuss life in terms of the ideal. The Conclusion to the *Renaissance* speaks rather of living intensely in the beautiful present. The essay on Wordsworth quiets this down to living in impassioned contemplation of man and of nature. It is not until the *Child in the House,* four years later, that we find life envisaged in terms of the ideal. Florean Deleal, the child in question, came to conceive of religion as an idealized representation of daily life, in the light of which we may orient the details of our existence.[2]

> His way of conceiving religion came then to be in effect what it ever afterwards remained—a sacred history indeed, but still more a sacred ideal, a transcendent version or representation, under intenser and more expressive light and shade, of human life and its familiar or exceptional incidents, birth, death, marriage, youth, age, tears, joy, rest, sleep, waking—a mirror, towards which men might turn away their eyes from vanity and dullness, and see themselves therein as angels, with their

---

[1] "Robert Elsmere," *Guardian,* p. 68; see also "Browne," *Appre.,* pp. 159–60; "Pascal," *passim, Misc. Studies; Gaston,* p. 113.
[2] In this essay the word 'ideal' is used in two senses: (1) meaning the abstract thought, as opposed to its "sensible vehicle" (*Misc. Studies,* p. 186); (2) meaning the 'type,' that is, the mental conception of the purified essence of the object (*ibid.,* pp. 179, 193–4). See *supra,* pp. 43–4.

daily meat and drink, even, become a kind of sacred transaction—a complementary strain or burden, applied to our every-day existence, whereby the stray snatches of music in it re-set themselves, and fall into the scheme of some higher and more consistent harmony.[1]

Pater calls this a "substitution of the typical for the actual."[2] He is now presenting, as the highest goal, that one should construct for oneself an imaginative world—the 'type,' or purified, 'rectified' essence of the real world, a 'vision' of the ideal—and live in it.

By the time he writes *Marius the Epicurean*, Pater has come to see everything in terms of the ideal. This mode of thought colors his whole account of Marius' development. He tells us that when Marius was a child, he began delightedly to live in his own idealized vision of the world.

> Those childish days of reverie, when he played at priests, played in many another day-dream, working his way from the actual present, as far as he might, with a delightful sense of escape in replacing the outer world of other people by an inward world as himself really cared to have it, had made him a kind of "idealist." He was become aware of the possibility of a large dissidence between an inward and somewhat exclusive world of vivid personal apprehension, and the unimproved, unheightened reality of the life of those about him.[3]

It was this which prepared the way for his Cyrenaic scepticism, and made him ready

> to concede, somewhat more easily than others, the first point of his new lesson, that the individual is to himself the measure

[1] *Misc. Studies,* pp. 193–4.   [3] I, 132–3.
[2] *Ibid.,* p. 194.

102

Life as an Art

of all things, and to rely on the exclusive certainty to himself
of his own impressions.[1]

It is this lesson also which it is the chief function of all higher
education to impart,

> the art, namely, of so relieving the ideal or poetic traits, the
> elements of distinction, in our everyday life—of so exclu-
> sively living in them—that the unadorned remainder of it,
> the mere drift or *débris* of our days, comes to be as though it
> were not.[2]

When Marius accepts the Cyrenaic ethics, he takes as his
goal to realize "the pleasure of the 'Ideal Now.'" This is to
be done by apprehending "the world in its fulness," and attaining "a vision, almost 'beatific,' of ideal personalities in life
and art." [3] The Stoic philosophy is presented in similar terms:
"It is in thy power to think as thou wilt," Marcus Aurelius
believed; and he frequently insisted on "the duty of thus making discreet, systematic use of the power of imaginative vision
for purposes of spiritual culture, 'since the soul takes colour
from its fantasies.'" [4]

The Christian philosophy finally fulfils most completely of
all the need of Marius. "That old longing for escape," "for a
lifting, from time to time, of the actual horizon," "had been
satisfied by this vision of the church in Cecilia's house, as never
before." [5] The highest point of all Marius' experience, his
vision of a Companion and Creator of the universe, he calls an
apprehension of "the *Great Ideal*"; and he says that that
hour of insight has made the world about him look further

[1] *Ibid.*
[2] I, 53-4.
[3] II, 21-2; see also I, 147-9.
[4] II, 38.
[5] II, 106.

off and less real than ever.[1] "Must not all that remained of life be but a search for the equivalent of that Ideal, among so-called actual things—a gathering together of every trace or token of it, which his actual experience might present?"[2] At the end of his life, summing it all up, Marius reflects:

> Revelation, vision, the discovery of a vision, the *seeing* of a perfect humanity, in a perfect world—through all his alternations of mind, by some dominant instinct, determined by the original necessities of his own nature and character, he had always set that above the *having*, or even the *doing*, of anything. For, such vision, if received with due attitude on his part, was, in reality, the *being* something, and as such was surely a pleasant offering or sacrifice to whatever gods there might be, observant of him. And how goodly had the vision been!—one long unfolding of beauty and energy in things, upon the closing of which he might gratefully utter his *"Vixi!"*[3]

In Pater's work after *Marius* there is never again such stress on living in the vision of the ideal, though there is a certain recurrence to it in *Plato and Platonism,* as would be natural in the discussion of that particular philosopher. In summing up Plato's doctrine Pater says, "Sanguine about any form of absolute knowledge, of eternal, or indefectible, or immutable truth, with our modern temperament as it is, we shall hardly become, even under the direction of Plato." But he "may yet promote in us what we call 'ideals'—the aspiration towards a more perfect Justice, a more perfect Beauty, physical and intellectual, a more perfect condition of human affairs, than any one has ever yet seen; that κοσμος, in which things *are* only as

[1] II, 71, 75.   [2] II, 72.   [3] II, 218.

they are *thought* by a perfect mind, to which experience is constantly approximating us, but which it does not provide." [1]

The entire growth in Pater's philosophy of life has been from youthful idealism to adolescent scepticism, back to idealism again. Such a growth was doubtless primarily due to an inborn idealistic bias, disturbed temporarily by the impact of a larger world, but reasserting itself in maturity. Miss Helen H. Young, in her useful study of *Walter Pater's Writings as a Reflection of British Philosophical Opinion, 1860–1890*, has shown that this natural change was reinforced by the current of philosophic thought of the time. In the 1860's, empiricism was the chief mode of English philosophical thought, under the influence of Hume, Comte, and Mill. In the 1870's, the current set strongly toward metaphysics, with much study of Kant and Hegel. Miss Young, though she has not given a full and ordered account of Pater's own development, has shown that most of the various elements of his thinking may be found scattered through the philosophical journals of his day. However that may be, whatever he picked up in his wide and discriminating reading he wove into the pattern of his own thought—from beginning to end viewing life as an art, seeking always to gain unity of spirit as well as richness of experience, gradually emphasizing more and more the elements of stability in the universe, coming finally to live in the vision of the ideal.

It is pertinent here to consider the soundness of Pater's philosophy of life. But first we must discard the common assumption that because he did not deal with the concrete problems of his own day, he was not concerned with life as it is. The truth is that he saw things in terms of the eternal

[1] P. 195.

rather than the temporal, and tried to present a way of life which should be good for every age. If his view of life is a wise one, it is the greater for being lifted above the particular problems of a particular day.

Standing off, then, to survey his philosophy, we see much of permanent value in it. Though in this perplexed century to live life as an art seems a goal far remote from the immediate need, the time will come, unless we are all wiped off this planet, when we must decide how best to live the life for which we are now fighting. Taking the long view, we must acknowledge that to live life as an art can be a stimulating ideal.

As for the means of achieving this aim, Pater is again far-sighted when he tells us, on the one hand, to be unceasingly sensitive to the best, refining the perceptive powers of our minds till every moment brings its contribution of riches; and on the other, to hold ourselves stable and poised within the unceasing whirl. His admonition to seize beauty wherever it may be found—in art, in nature, in human character—is surely valuable; and so is his advice to penetrate within the imperfections of the world and to construct for oneself a vision of the ideal, the world as it might be. His pity for the sufferings of humanity shows a concern reaching out beyond the narrow confines of himself.

Pater's philosophy, however, breaks down at the point where it emphasizes *"being,* rather than *doing."* In his youth he seemed to recommend perceiving and feeling rather than doing. Later, when his idealism was fully developed, he taught "the *seeing* of a perfect humanity in a perfect world"—living in one's vision of the ideal. Whether or not this is essentially sound depends on what is meant by living in the ideal. If it

Life as an Art

means endeavoring in every way to live up to the ideal qualities of character which one has envisaged, or endeavoring to bring the real world closer to the ideal, that is one thing; but if it means escaping to a world of dreams that is quite another. We must regretfully conclude that Pater's "ideal" was an escape rather than a stimulus. Even his pity for humanity never led him to any active alleviation of its sufferings.

This is not a necessary consequence of his other doctrines, however. It is a result rather of his passive temperament, dependent on what shaping forces of heredity and environment we do not know. The love of beauty does not necessarily bring in its train either inhumanity or inaction. Ruskin and Morris, along with many others, bear witness to the fact that a life spent in the service of beauty can also be a life spent in the service of mankind. Life as an art might be made a doctrine worthy of an active soul. With Pater it was a consoling dream.

CHAPTER IV

Aesthetic Criticism

I. THE CRITIC'S DUTY: TO FIND THE FORMULA

SINCE WALTER PATER is primarily a critic, all lines of inquiry must finally converge at his conception of the critical function. This conception is amazingly consistent and well defined from the beginning to the end of his work. When he gathered together several essays already written and published them in 1873 under the title *Studies in the History of the Renaissance,* he formulated a preface to explain his critical theories. There he tells us that the main duty of the critic is to disengage the peculiar essence of each creative artist's work, to analyze and reduce to its elements the 'special, unique impression of pleasure' produced by each individual work of art.

> The function of the aesthetic critic is to distinguish, to analyse, and separate from its adjuncts, the virtue by which a picture, a landscape, a fair personality in life or in a book, produces this special impression of beauty or pleasure, to indicate what the source of that impression is, and under what conditions it is experienced. His end is reached when he has disengaged that virtue, and noted it, as a chemist notes some natural element, for himself and others.[1]

The relation of this aim to Pater's fundamental metaphysic is shown in the first paragraph of the Preface, where he says

[1] Pp. ix, x.

Aesthetic Criticism

that it is not the duty of the critic to evolve an abstract definition of beauty, but to find "the formula which expresses most
adequately this or that special manifestation of it."[1] As has
been seen, he has a strong faith in empiricism, inductive
science, and denies any transcendental reality. He is therefore
not interested, like Coleridge, in judging literature deduc-
tively, according to whether it is true to a reality manifesting
itself in nature.[2] He believes that "Beauty, like all other qualities presented to human experience, is relative."[3] The critic
must therefore proceed inductively. His aim will not be to see to
what extent a work of art conforms to some absolute standard;
it will be to analyze each particular manifestation of beauty,
to note fine distinctions, to define the individual.

He gives his theory its most condensed expression when he
says that he attempts to find the 'formula' of a given writer.
This phrase is used in the Preface,[4] and several times later, as
when he finds the 'formula' of Mérimée to be enthusiasm "for
rude, crude, naked force in men and women wherever it could
be found; himself carrying ever, as a mask, the conventional
attire of the modern world."[5] That his main critical purpose

[1] Pp. vii–viii.
[2] Cf. Coleridge: "I should call that investigation fair and philosophical, in which the critic announces and endeavors to establish the principles,
which he holds for the foundation of poetry in general, with the specifica-
tion of these in their application to the different *classes* of poetry. Having
thus prepared his canons of criticism for praise and condemnation, he would
proceed to particularize the most striking passages to which he deems them
applicable, faithfully noting the frequent or infrequent recurrence of
similar merits or defects. . . . Then if his premises be rational, his deduc-
tions legitimate, and his conclusions justly applied, the reader, and possibly
the poet himself, may adopt his judgment in the light of judgment and
in the independence of free-agency." *Biographia Literaria* (ed. Shawcross), II, 85.
[3] P. vii.   [4] P. vii.   [5] *Misc. Studies*, p. 14.

is to discover and to formulate for others the essence of each artist's genius is indicated repeatedly. For instance, in his study of Botticelli, he inquires, "What is the peculiar sensation, what is the peculiar quality of pleasure, which his work has the property of exciting in us, and which we cannot get elsewhere?" [1]

Such an aim is certainly objective, requiring careful, analytical thinking. And Pater, in his own criticism, adheres to it with remarkable fidelity. In almost all of his major essays, he attempts to analyze and convey the essence, the unique quality, of the artist's work. This is true from his very first critical essay, the study of Coleridge's metaphysics, where he finds the 'active principle' of Coleridge to be his 'quest for the absolute.' It is true in every essay in the *Renaissance.* For instance, the 'formula' of Winckelmann is his Greek temperament, which Pater carefully defines. When he comes to Michelangelo, Pater takes the accepted definition of the great painter's main quality as strength—"a wonderful strength, verging, as in the things of the imagination great strength always does, on what is singular or strange," [2]—and shows that it alone is not adequate to define his genius, for along with strength there is also sweetness.

In his later work, Pater did not follow as undeviatingly the plan of separating out the essence. He wrote a number of anonymous reviews of novels, in which he usually devoted his

---

[1] *Ren.,* pp. 50–1; see also "Two Early French Stories," *Ren.,* p. 19; "Leonardo," *ibid.,* p. 109; "Du Bellay," *ibid.,* p. 167; "Winckelmann," *ibid.,* p. 178; "Amiel's Journal," *Guardian,* 25–6; "Mérimée,' *Misc. Studies,* p. 14; "Mr. George Moore," *passim, Sketches and Reviews; Plato and Platonism,* pp. 124–5.

[2] P. 73.

attention to the main characters presented. Three of the essays in *Appreciations—Rossetti, Lamb,* and *Sir Thomas Browne—* are not organized around the 'active principle.' But they are Pater's only major criticisms of individual men not so organized. To the very end he is still searching for the 'formula.' In his last book he finds that of Plato to be his "sensuous love of the unseen." [1]

Usually to Pater, finding the central quality of an artist's work means a psychological analysis, finding the central quality of his temperament which of course manifested itself in his work—as the 'active principle' of Leonardo was his union of curiosity with the desire for beauty. This logically follows from Pater's theory, previously set forth, that each mind has the power of imposing a unity of its own upon the fleeting phenomena of the universe.[2] The point in criticism will naturally be to get at the 'active principle' of each mind, which places a unique, individual stamp upon every one of its creations.

Very often, though not always, Pater recounts the life of an artist, so handling it as to show what relation it bore at every point to the writer's 'active principle.' He does this, for instance, in the essays on Leonardo, Michelangelo, and Winckelmann. In such cases he works from a very thorough study of sources. Benson tells us:

> Any one who has ever gone over the same ground as Pater, and studied the same authorities, will be amazed to find how conscientiously and diligently the material has all been employed; not by elaborately amplifying detail, but by condensing an abundance of scattered points into a single illu-

---

[1] *Plato and Platonism,* pp. 143, 140.   [2] See *supra,* pp. 88–90.

111

minating hint, a poignant image, an apt illustration. . . . Not to travel far for instances, the essay on Leonardo is a perfect example of this. The writing is so delicate, so apparently fanciful, that it is only through a careful study of the available tradition that one comes to realize how minute is the knowledge that furnishes out these gemmed and luminous sentences.[1]

Any one who needs to be convinced of Pater's care for accurate information should consult Staub's analysis of *The Prince of Court Painters*. Pater calls this an 'Imaginary Portrait' of Watteau, and does not even pretend to be offering an authentic biographical sketch. But Staub's footnotes show what authorities he has relied on for each detail, and with what fidelity he has followed them.[2] He has studied the best sources of information, and woven them together skilfully, adhering closely to the facts, and at the same time trying to penetrate to the motives which lay underneath them. He has done exactly what is attempted by writers of the modern school of biography; and though he claims only to be writing an *Imaginary Portrait,* has taken scarcely any more liberties than they do. The major liberty taken is to have the whole story told in a diary written by a young girl who is imagined to be in love with Watteau. The description of Watteau's paintings is extraordinarily successful in catching their exact atmosphere. And as usual, the 'formula' emerges from the whole. Watteau "was always a seeker after something in the world that is there in no satisfying measure or not at all." [3] He was able to paint so beautifully the Paris world of fashion, with all its delicate

[1] *Walter Pater,* p. 211.
[2] *Das imaginäre Porträt Walter Paters,* pp. 60–70.
[3] P. 44.

112

trivialities, because he painted into it something he knew was not there, the fairy-like, ideal, unspotted world of his boyhood dreams.

His research into the subjects about which he writes by no means proves Pater a great scholar. His knowledge was not profound. But in both his critical and his imaginative writing he knew how to make bare facts live again with their human significance. He had the imaginative power to vivify what he knew.

It is interesting to ask how successful Pater has been in finding the 'active principle' of each artist. Different people would give different replies. Paul Elmer More, for instance, would have said that Pater was almost never right; that he was always misled by his own temperament into presenting a distorted picture.[1] On the other hand, Hugh Walker, one of the best present-day students of nineteenth-century literature, tells us that "Pater was unusually well endowed with both the emotional and the intellectual gifts of the critic. There are few whose judgments are deserving of closer attention."[2] A. J. Farmer holds, discerningly, that Pater seldom attempted a written criticism except where some temperamental similarity allowed him to enter completely into the spirit of the work, and that such a complete identification with the author en-

[1] "The simple truth is that Pater was in no proper sense of the word a critic. He did not on the one hand from his own fixed point of view judge the great movements of history and the great artists in their reality; nor on the other hand did he show any dexterity in changing his own point of view and entering sympathetically into other moods than his own. To him history was only an extension of his own Ego, and he saw himself whithersoever he turned his eyes." "Walter Pater," *Shelburne Essays,* Series VIII, p. 99.

[2] *Cambridge History of English Literature* (ed. Ward and Waller, Cambridge, 1917), XIV, 175.

abled him to give a strikingly penetrating and sound analysis.[1] The objective validity of the essays certainly varies. One could hardly ask for sounder treatments than those of *Wordsworth, Luca della Robbia, Joachim du Bellay, Measure for Measure,* or *Shakespeare's English Kings.* The essay on Raphael, on the other hand, is so inadequate as to be almost humorous. Studies such as those on Botticelli, Michelangelo, and the genius of Plato set forth 'formulas' whose objective validity is a matter of debate.

It is impossible to say definitely that Pater derived his critical aim of seeking the 'formula,' the 'active principle,' from any particular predecessor. No important English critic before him had announced that definite purpose in criticism. Many critics have said in passing that each great artist has his own peculiar individuality. But Pater is exceptional in announcing his intention as the definition of that individuality in a brief formula, and in regularly organizing his essays to bring out that definition.

It is interesting, however, to find a decided similarity in Baudelaire. In criticizing Eugène Delacroix, Baudelaire says:

> Je crois, Monsieur, que l'important ici est simplement de chercher la qualité caractéristique du génie de Delacroix et d'essayer de la définir; de chercher en quoi il diffère de ses plus illustres devanciers, tout en les égalant . . . en un mot, de quelle *spécialité* la Providence avait chargé Eugène Delacroix dans le développement historique de la Peinture.[2]

Then he goes on to define as carefully as he can *la spécialité* of

[1] *Walter Pater as a Critic of English Literature, passim.*
[2] Delacroix, sa vie et son oeuvre," *L'art romantique,* Oeuvres, IV, 166–7.

Delacroix. In another place he uses Pater's very word, 'formula'; for he says, "Je tourmente mon esprit pour en arracher quelque formule qui exprime bien la *spécialité* d'Eugène Delacroix." [1] To Baudelaire as to Pater, this meant an interest in the temperament and aims of the artist:

> La critique doit chercher plutôt à pénétrer intimement le tempérament de chaque artiste et les mobiles qui le font agir, qu'à analyser, à raconter chaque oeuvre minitieusement. [2]

This is not to say that Pater borrowed the idea of the 'formula' or the phrase itself from Baudelaire. We have no direct evidence that he read any of Baudelaire's criticisms; and his two references to the French poet do not occur till rather late. [3]

The critics that Pater seemed to admire most were Lamb, Arnold, and Sainte-Beuve. When he was training himself in composition, he translated a page every day for months from the latter. [4] Sainte-Beuve did not attempt to find any 'formula' to cover a given man, but he did try to elucidate the man's essential character by giving every detail of biography or background that would shed light on it. He, like Pater, was interested in defining the temperament of the author which shaped his work.

One of Pater's best essays is about Lamb, whom he admires both as a man and as a critic. Much of Lamb's criticism is in

---

[1] "Salon de 1859," *Curiosités esthétiques,* Oeuvres, V, 268.

[2] "Exposition universelle de 1855," *Curiosités esthétiques,* Oeuvres, V, 208.

[3] In *Gaston de Latour,* 1888, he uses the phrase "flowers of evil" (p. 71); and in the essay on Mérimée, 1890, he speaks of the exaggeration of Baudelaire's art (*Misc. Studies,* p. 13). He is said to have read Poe in Baudelaire's translation (Benson, p. 23). See *supra,* p. 19.

[4] Sharp, "Personal Reminiscences of Walter Pater," *Atlantic,* LXXIV (Dec. 1894), 806.

the form of notes, elucidating points about the Elizabethan plays he was editing. But his longer studies he organized around the central quality of the work he was discussing. For instance, the essay on Restoration Comedy dwelt on its quality of unreality, of escape from the real world into the lightsome world of Cuckoldom. But where Pater concentrated on the temperament or aim of the artist, Lamb concentrated more on the work of art. With Pater, we infer the character of the work from what is said about the artist. With Lamb, we infer the character of the artist from what is said about the work. What Pater absorbed from Lamb was probably not a method, but a goal—the goal of sympathetic, penetrating interpretation.

Echoes of Arnold, both in phrase and idea, appear constantly throughout Pater's work. Arnold, in some of his best critiques, sums up what he considers the essential character of the artist under discussion, and organizes his entire essay to bring out that character. He sees Heine, for instance, as a "brave soldier in the Liberation War of humanity"; Maurice Guerin as one who has a magical faculty of interpreting nature; and Marcus Aurelius as a teacher of morality suffused with emotion.[1] Pater acknowledges Arnold's goal as his own when he says that the aim of criticism is "to see the object as in itself it really is."[2] But Arnold does not proclaim his intention of summing up the essence of each particular artist, nor does he direct most of his criticisms to that end. If Pater learned from him to seek the 'formula,' he gave that objective a

[1] *Essays in Criticism,* 1st Series.
[2] "Preface," *Ren.,* p. viii. Cf. Arnold, *On Translating Homer,* Works, V, 217.

definite phrasing, as Arnold did not, and followed it more consistently than his teacher.

Though Pater's purpose was to find the essence of the given artist, it is a mistake to ignore his interest in the historical setting and implications of a work of art. This study of his theory has already shown that he looked on art as expressing not only the man but the age.[1] It is odd, considering its prominence, that commentators have so largely neglected this aspect of his work. For while he makes no addition to our store of scholarship, he does show in his criticism a lively historic interest. Consider the *Renaissance,* for instance. Although these essays are not a systematic attempt to trace the origins or the characteristics of the Renaissance, they do, in discussing various artists, illuminate some of the most important features of "that complex, many-sided movement." [2] Pater has given us, first, the very beginnings of the Renaissance within the middle ages as it bloomed in France; here two delightful romances exemplify "the more liberal and comely way of conceiving life," shown particularly in the growing claim for the full play of human affection. He treats next several phases of the full Renaissance: Pico della Mirandola illustrates the attempt of the new philosophy to reconcile the ancient Greek religion with Christianity. But religions, Pater says, cannot be reconciled in the allegorical fashion attempted by Pico, but only by an understanding of their historic development, "as so many stages in the gradual education of the human mind." Botticelli and Leonardo da Vinci illustrate the typical Renaissance desire to embody in line and color "the true complexion of humanity." The 'School of Giorgione' is the Venetian

[1] See *supra,* pp. 36–8. [2] P. xi.

117

school of painting, which apprehended more unerringly than any other "the necessary limitations of the art of painting," and "the essence of what is pictorial in a picture." Luca della Robbia is contrasted with Michelangelo as each endeavors with his own special technique of sculpture to express individual character and feeling. Michelangelo expresses the Platonic love tradition in his poetry (an English translation of which had just appeared when Pater wrote); his painting and sculpture have a combination of strength and sweetness which represents both the best of the middle ages and the best of the new flowering. The essay on Joachim du Bellay takes us back to France, where the series of essays began, and shows the exquisite elegance which is yet the decadence of the late Renaissance. Pater adds an essay on the eighteenth-century Germany scholar, Winckelmann, explaining its presence by saying that Winckelmann was in sympathy with the earliest humanists, and could be called "the last fruit of the Renaissance."

Through this early volume and in all his work, Pater is interested in the fashion in which one period or school of art develops into another. He makes the point, for instance, that there was no clear-cut division between the Renaissance and the middle ages, but that the one was foreshadowed in the other. The essay on Luca della Robbia is one of the best from the standpoint of an historical interest in art development. It takes Della Robbia as representative of the fifteenth-century Tuscan sculptors, and their system of giving life, breath, and expression to the hard outlines of sculpture by a system of low relief. In comparison with this method, Pater discusses the method of the Greeks and that of Michelangelo for achieving the same result. The Greeks avoided the appearance of hardness and caricature by seeing the type in the individual, purging "from the individual all that belongs only to him, all the accidents, the feelings and actions of the special moment, all that . . . is apt to look like a frozen thing if one arrests it." [1] Michelangelo was not satisfied with this system of abstraction, which could not bring what was inward in the soul to the surface, and he "secured for his work individuality and intensity of expression," and avoided "a too heavy realism" by a suggestive incompleteness in his figures.[2]

Throughout his work Pater is particularly interested in great tendencies of human thought, and he likes to treat individual men as detailed illustrations of these great tendencies. For instance, he sees Winckelmann as representing the recurrent return of civilization to the Greek tradition to be clarified and corrected by it.[3] Coleridge is to him one of the long succession of philosophers who have set out in "quest of the absolute." Very skilfully though briefly, he sets Coleridge's metaphysical theory in its place in the history of philosophy, showing its relation to Plato, the Neo-Platonists, and the German transcendentalists.[4]

The *Greek Studies* are a series of historical essays discussing the growth of Greek mythology from very early nature myths, and the various periods of development in Greek sculpture. Two studies in the book, *The Bacchanals of Euripides* and *Hippolytus Veiled,* are interpretations of particular plays. The other essays in mythology are organized around separate myths, but deal with their historical origins and significance.

[1] *Ren.,* p. 66.
[2] *Ibid.,* p. 67.
[3] *Ibid.,* pp. 198-9.
[4] "Coleridge," *Appre.,* pp. 65-9, 73-9, 81-3.

The Aesthetic of Walter Pater

The essays on sculpture are not organized around individual men, but around periods and tendencies, and are packed with historical information.

But though Pater, when he criticizes particular men, takes into account their historical setting, he is less interested in that than in their individual genius. The essays in *Plato and Platonism* set forth with beautiful clarity his exact position. "All true criticism of philosophic doctrine," he tells us, "as of every other product of human mind, must begin with an historic estimate of the conditions antecedent and contemporary, which helped to make it precisely what it was." But he goes on to say that while there is on one side the "fatal, irresistible, mechanic play" of circumstances to be analyzed and explained, "there is also, as if acting from the opposite side, the comparatively inexplicable force of a personality resistant to, while it is molded by, them." And then he sets forth the philosophy of his own criticism:

> It might even be said that the trial-task of criticism, in regard to literature and art no less than to philosophy, begins exactly where the estimate of general conditions, of the conditions common to all the products of this or that particular age—of the "environment"—leaves off, and we touch what is unique in the individual genius which contrived after all, by force of will, to have its own masterful way with that environment.[1]

His composition of *Plato and Platonism* is a striking illustration of his own theory. The first essay written was the one called *The Genius of Plato,* in which he attempted what he considered the task of primary importance, to analyze the

[1] Pp. 124-5.

120

'active principle' of Plato. But when he came to present a whole series of essays on Plato, he started with the historical background, considering first the elements from preceding philosophies which Plato took up into his work, and exactly what he made of them. He showed also other influential relationships: that of Socrates and Plato; that of Plato and the Sophists. Then, having spent five chapters on the historical background, he inserted the chapter first written, *The Genius of Plato,* and considered the individual, unique characteristic of Plato's mind which determined the final character of his work. In other words, if Pater took time to write a book about a man, he would start with the historical background. If he was writing only a single essay, he took the background pretty much for granted, and proceeded at once to the more important task, that of analyzing the prime characteristic of the author's work.

2. THE MEANING OF THE TERM 'AESTHETIC CRITIC'

Pater's true aims in criticism have been considerably obscured by his use of the term 'aesthetic.' The foregoing account of his purpose now makes it possible to clear away a misunderstanding. When Pater called himself by the title 'aesthetic critic,' he was borrowing a common philosophic word and using it in its technical sense. 'Aesthetic' comes from a Greek word, "of or pertaining to αἰσθητά, things perceptible by the senses." The term was first applied by the German philosopher Baumgarten about 1750 to the science or philosophy of the criticism of taste. He considered that beauty was the perfection of sensuous knowledge, *i.e.,* of feeling or sensation; and so with him 'aesthetic' came to be connected both

The Aesthetic of Walter Pater

with sensations and with the philosophy of beauty.[1] It retained that association through most of succeeding philosophy. Aesthetic came to be known as "the philosophy or theory of taste, or of the perception of the beautiful." [2] It retained its connection with sensation, since beauty comes to us directly through sense perception. Pater keeps close to the original derivation of the word when he says that the aesthetic critic "regards all the objects with which he has to do . . . as powers or forces producing pleasurable sensations." [3] Philosophers differed, however, as to whether the beauty with which aesthetics deals is the beauty of art and nature, or only of art. Hegel confined it definitely to art.[4] The more usual application, made for instance by the English aesthetic philosophers, Herbert Spencer and Grant Allen, included the beauty of nature as well.[5] Pater followed the latter usage. In the Preface he says that the objects with which aesthetic criticism deals are "all works of art, and the fairer forms of nature and human life." [6]

Besides its philosophic meaning, there was another obvious reason why Pater might use the term 'aesthetic.' He could not call himself a literary critic, for he was equally interested in painting and sculpture; nor an art critic, for that would seem to leave out literature. What term was there comprehensive enough to describe him but 'aesthetic critic,' one who was concerned with beauty in all its forms?

[1] Bosanquet, *History of Aesthetic* (London, 1904), p. 184.
[2] New English Dictionary.
[3] *Ren.,* p. ix.
[4] *Intro.* (trs. Bosanquet), pp. 38–41.
[5] See Spencer, *Principles of Psychology,* II, pt. 9, ch. 9, and Allen, *Physiological Aesthetics* (New York, 1877), ch. 3.
[6] *Ren.,* p. ix.

Aesthetic Criticism

Unfortunately, however, not every one understood the word 'aesthetic' in its philosophic sense. The popular mind has usually taken it to imply an appreciation merely of the formal aspects of art, or an exaggerated sensibility to beautiful objects with no intellectual basis for one's appreciation. Some, even in high places, have used it in an unphilosophic sense. Ruskin, for instance, said, "Now the term 'aesthesis' properly signifies mere sensual perception of the outward qualities and necessary effects of bodies." [1] And he thought that when we call the faculty of the mind to which art appeals 'aesthetic,' we degrade it "to a mere operation of sense, . . . so that the arts which appeal to it sink into a mere amusement, ministers to morbid sensibilities, ticklers and fanners of the soul's sleep." [2]

Used with that meaning, as it often is, 'aesthetic' conveys an entirely misleading impression of Pater's work. In saying that all beautiful objects are to be regarded as "powers or forces producing pleasurable sensations," he certainly did not mean to confine sensation, as did Ruskin, to a "mere sensual perception of the outward qualities and necessary effects of bodies"; nor was he interested only in form. He was, to be sure, unusually susceptible to sensuous beauty. Like Florean Deleal he early felt "a passionateness in his relation to fair outward objects, an inexplicable excitement in their presence, which disturbed him, and from which he half longed to be free." In his childhood he felt "a certain, at times seemingly exclusive, predominance in his interests, of beautiful physical things, a kind of tyranny of the senses over him." [3] These

[1] *Modern Painters,* II, pt. III, sec. 1, ch. 2, § 1, Works, IV, 42.
[2] *Ibid.,* II, pt. III, sec. 1, ch. 1, § 10, Works, IV, 35–6.
[3] "Child in the House," *Misc. Studies,* p. 186.

characteristics he shared with the whole art for art's sake group. Gautier had said, in the person of his hero Alphonse,

> J'adore sur toutes choses la beauté de la forme. . . . Il y a certaines ondulations de contours, certaines finesses de lèvres, certaines coupes de paupières, certaines inclinaisons de tête, certains allongements d'ovales qui me ravissent au delà de toute expression et m'attachent pendant des heures entières.[1]

Gautier had credited himself with the sin of *concupiscentia oculorum,* or the "lust of the eye," as Pater was later to say.[2] His phrase was seized upon as descriptive of the whole group when he called himself "one for whom the sensible world existed." [3]

But though Pater possessed that inescapable necessity for a true art critic, an intense appreciation of sensible beauty, his conception of criticism involved much more than that. The critic, he says in the Preface to the *Renaissance,* must inquire of each beautiful object, "How is my nature modified by its presence, and under its influence?" [4] And then for an example of the quality of a writer which produces a "pleasurable sensation" in the reader, he cites Wordsworth's "strange, mystical sense of a life in natural things, and of man's life as a part

---

[1] *Mlle. de Maupin* (Paris, 1924), ch. V, p. 146.

[2] In *L'Artiste,* Dec. 1856, Gautier wrote: "L'Ecriture parle quelque part de la concupiscence des yeux, *concupiscentia oculorum*:— ce péché est notre péché, et nous espérons que Dieu nous le pardonnera." Cf. Pater: "the activity in him of a more than customary sensuousness, 'the lust of the eye,' as the Preacher says, which might lead him, one day, how far!" "The Child in the House," *Misc. Studies,* p. 181.

[3] Pater refers to this characterization of Gautier in *Plato and Platonism,* p. 126.

[4] P. viii.

of nature." [1] His reasons for choosing the Italian Renaissance for study in his first volume are revealing:

> It is in Italy, in the fifteenth century, that the interest of the Renaissance mainly lies,—in that solemn fifteenth century which can hardly be studied too much, not merely for its positive results in the things of the intellect and the imagination, its concrete works of art, its special and prominent personalities, with their profound aesthetic charm, but for its general spirit and character, for the ethical qualities of which it is a consummate type. [2]

The critic, Pater holds, must search always for the best. He must ask, "In whom did the stir, the genius, the sentiment of the period find itself? where was the receptacle of its refinement, its elevation, its taste?" [3] So the critic is definitely to judge of the best of each period, to separate it out for study. That is what Pater actually does himself. He seldom deals in unfavorable judgments; but his choice of subject matter is in itself a judgment. He is particularly interested in discussing the greatest periods in art—the age of Greece, the Renaissance, and the nineteenth century. And within the great periods he deals largely with the great figures. Not wholly, however. In the *Renaissance* he makes apology for including so minor a figure as Botticelli. Besides the great men, he says,

> there is a certain number of artists who have a distinct faculty of their own by which they convey to us a peculiar quality of pleasure which we cannot get elsewhere; and these too have their place in general culture, and must be interpreted to it by those who have felt their charm strongly. [4]

[1] P. xi.
[2] P. xiii.
[3] P. x.
[4] P. 61.

In pursuance of this principle, he occasionally writes book reviews of distinctly minor modern authors, whom he wishes to interpret to the public.

In choosing artists to discuss, Pater is drawn only to those whose view on life seems to him humanely valuable. Lamb, for instance, he admires for his humor, pity, and critical appreciation, all of which flow from his boundless sympathy, the power of identifying himself with whatever he is writing about, whether it be the Elizabethan dramatists, or life in its small but infinitely touching sorrows and joys. Mérimée he finds significant for his insight into dynamic personality. Pascal is the supreme example of a religious soul always beset by the sword points of doubt and always holding them at bay. Rossetti's poetry unveils "the ideal aspects of common things," but still more, it creates imaginatively "things that are ideal from their very birth." [1] Even in his early work Pater uses the same criterion. Leonardo he considers valuable because he delves into the secret places of nature and human nature, seizing their innermost secrets; and Winckelmann illustrates in his own life the power of art to help the soul gain unity and stability, in "blitheness and repose."

Throughout his work Pater appreciates, not so much the truthful portrayal of every variety of emotion, as the presentation of the nobler, more generous emotions. The medieval romance, *The Friendship of Amis and Amile,* for instance, is the story of a great friendship, "pure and generous, pushed to a sort of passionate exaltation, and more than faithful unto death." [2] And again, Michelangelo's *Pieta* is the expression of the noble Florentine attitude toward death, seeing it in its

[1] *Appre.,* p. 218. [2] *Ren.,* p. 8.

quiet distinction, and "with a sentiment of profound pity."[1] In his anonymous reviews of novels, Pater is concerned almost wholly with the worth of the personages portrayed; the plots are important only as they help to form worthy character. Of Feuillet he says, characteristically, "Often, his most attentive reader will have forgotten the actual details of his plot; while the soul, tried, enlarged, shaped by it, remains as a well-fixed type in the memory."[2]

But while Pater is particularly interested in the presentation of the nobler emotions and more worthy characters, that does not mean that he is able to appreciate only the prettified. Dante, Goethe, and Victor Hugo were the names which came most often from his pen. His words about Victor Hugo give us the clue to his general attitude. He says that Winckelmann, with all his appreciation of Greek art, "could hardly have conceived of the subtle and penetrative, yet somewhat grotesque art of the modern world. What would he have thought of Gilliatt, in Victor Hugo's *Travailleurs de la Mer,* or of the bleeding mouth of Fantine in the first part of *Les Misérables,* penetrated as those books are with a sense of beauty, as lively and transparent as that of a Greek?"[3] When we remember that Fantine had become a street walker and had sold everything she possessed, even her own teeth, in order to care for her daughter, we know that her bleeding mouth as she sang her dying lullaby symbolized the most sacrificial mother-love. And

---

[1] *Ibid.,* p. 94.

[2] *Appre.,* pp. 219–20.

[3] *Ren.,* p. 223. This would appear to bespeak an acquaintance with Hugo's theory of the grotesque, set forth particularly in his Preface to *Cromwell,* but it is only a passing reference. Pater gives us no developed aesthetic of the ugly.

we see that Pater accepted such a portrayal of the cruelties and ugliness of life for the sake of the nobility of character which it revealed.

This interpretation is borne out by his further remark that modern art "deals confidently and serenely with life, conflict, evil." [1] Modern man feels himself entangled in the web of an intricate universal law revealed to him by science. "Natural laws we shall never modify, embarrass us as they may; but there is still something in the nobler or less noble attitude with which we watch their fatal combinations." [2] The romances of Goethe and Victor Hugo show us groups of noble men and women working out of their tragic situation a supreme *Dénouement*.

Ugly realism or naturalism, however, Pater found distasteful. He speaks of the "somewhat artificial modern preference for telling and having a story in all its harsh unrelieved effect." [3] His praise of Lemaitre's *Serenus* is revealing: "Its union of realism, of the force of style which is allied to a genuine realism, with an entire freedom from the dubious interests of almost all French fiction, gives it a charming freshness of effect." [4] He prefers Fabre to Zola, though he acknowledges Zola's "undoubted power." [5] He puts one of Symons' poems below the rest,

> for the same reason which makes me put Rossetti's 'Jenny,' and some of Browning's pathetic-satiric pieces, below the rank which many assign them. In no one of the poems I

[1] *Ibid.,* p. 223.
[2] *Ibid.,* p. 231.
[3] "A Poet with Something to Say," *Sketches and Reviews,* pp. 139–40.
[4] *Sketches and Reviews,* p. 22.
[5] "Ferdinand Fabre," *Guardian,* p. 121.

am thinking of, is the inherent sordidness of everything in the persons supposed, except the one poetic trait then under treatment, quite forgotten.[1]

To Pater realism meant naturalness, convincingness, and not a stress on the less agreeable aspects of life.

In summary, then, Pater is not an aesthetic critic in the popular sense of the term: he does not have an exaggerated sensibility to beautiful objects with no intellectual basis for his appreciation; he is not moved merely by the formal aspects of art; he is not without high standards of human worth. Actually, he is an aesthetic critic in that he is intelligently interested in all forms of beauty, including the beauties of the human spirit.

3. 'IMPRESSIONISM'

There is a second misconception about Pater's work which remains to be dealt with. Not only is he condemned by the adjective 'aesthetic,' but he is also praised or denounced as 'impressionistic.' The word 'impressionism' is used at the present time in two senses, frequently not clearly distinguished. It may mean a reasonably objective attempt to analyze the central impression of an artist's work, the impression it might be expected to make on any sensitive, cultivated observer. In this more objective sense of the word there is no doubt that Pater is an impressionist. His aim of finding the 'formula' makes him distinctly that; he is trying to discover the special quality which accounts for the particular impression made by each individual artist's work.

[1] Letter to Symons, quoted in Symons' "Walter Pater," *Figures of Several Centuries* (New York, [1916]), p. 326.

The Aesthetic of Walter Pater

But the term 'impressionism' may also be used in a much more subjective sense, as meaning the attempt of the critic to give merely his own personal reactions to a work of art, however whimsical or fanciful they may be, rather than a reasoned judgment which would have validity for others. The Humanists employ the word in this sense. They believe that the impressionist is not really a critic at all, but a creator, or a would-be creator. Norman Foerster, for instance, tells us:

> The impressionist, in a word, may be defined as a disil-lusioned romantic critic who has turned creator. If he can-not see artistic objects as they are, if he cannot return to the impressions which the artist sought to objectify, if he cannot comprehend the uniqueness of artists, he can yet create new artistic objects by expressing his impression of the objects created by artists, and thus offer his own uniqueness in lieu of that of so-called creative artists.[1]

T. S. Eliot agrees with him,[2] and both use Pater as an illustration. Paul Elmer More, though he does not use the word 'impressionist,' is particularly bitter against Pater as a critic who falsifies everything he touches.[3] Irving Babbitt compares Pater to that arch-impressionist, Anatole France,[4] who said that "objective criticism has no more existence than has objective art. . . . To be quite frank, the critic ought to say: 'Gentlemen, I am going to speak about myself apropos of Shake-

---

[1] "The Impressionists," *Bookman,* LXX (Dec. 1929), 341.
[2] "The Perfect Critic," *The Sacred Wood* (London, 1920), pp. 2–3.
[3] "Walter Pater," *Shelburne Essays,* Series VIII, *passim.*
[4] *Masters of Modern French Criticism* (New York, 1912), p. 321 (see 317–20) ; see also "Impressionist versus Judicial Criticism," *PMLA,* XXI (1906), 687–705.

speare, apropos of Racine, or of Pascal, or of Goethe.' . . .
The good critic is he who relates the adventures of his own soul
among masterpieces." [1]

No doubt Pater very occasionally fits such a definition of
the impressionistic critic. He sometimes attempts to convey
to the reader by word-pictures and subtle suggestion the effect,
the 'impression,' produced by the work of art before him, and
in so doing creates something quite different. Take for instance the essay on Leonardo da Vinci. Everyone is familiar
with the long description beginning, "The presence that rose
thus so strangely beside the waters, is expressive of what in
the ways of a thousand years men had come to desire." [2]
Pater is reproducing the impression made on him, and reproducing it in another medium. The result is completely personal. Furthermore, the whole essay on Leonardo is filled
with phrases which reinforce the impression he is trying to
convey of a strange, subtle grace—such phrases as "a life of
brilliant sins and exquisite amusements," or "the smiling of
women and the motion of great waters," or "the portrait of
Beatrice d'Este, . . . precise and grave, full of the refinement
of the dead, in sad earth-coloured raiment, set with pale stones."

This method Pater may perhaps have learned from Swinburne, for Swinburne used it very often in his early work.
Compare, for instance, his description of one of Hugo's characters, a "virgin harlot":

> She has no more in common with the lewd low hirelings of
> the baser school of realism than a creature of the brothel
> and the street has in common with the Maenads who rent in

[1] *La vie littéraire* (Paris, 4th ed., 1889), Series I, pp. iii, iv.
[2] *Ren.*, pp. 124–5.

sunder the living limbs of Orpheus. We seem to hear about her the beat and clash of the terrible timbrels, the music that Aeschylus set to verse, the music that made mad, the upper notes of the psalm shrill and strong as a sea-wind, the 'bull-voiced' bellowing under-song of those dread choristers from somewhere out of sight, the tempest of tambourines giving back thunder to the thunder, the fury of divine lust that thickened with human blood the hill-streams of Cithaeron.[1]

The whole essay is in a similar vein.

But actually, only a small proportion of Pater's work deserves to be called impressionistic in the sense above adopted. Undoubtedly the *Botticelli* falls in this class. More than half of it is woven out of a fabric that almost everyone would agree to call personal, even fanciful. In the *Leonardo,* there are two pages out of twenty-six which are definitely impressionistic. But it is hard to find other essays of Pater with any considerable impressionistic element; and even the *Leonardo* is made up mostly of careful objective analysis rather than of personal reaction. After the *Renaissance,* impressionism in this sense is almost entirely absent from Pater's work. Many of his later critical writings took the form of anonymous book reviews, which are in no way distinctive. In the later essays published under his signature, he is still, for the most part, searching for the 'formula'; and in these he makes no use of the subjective type of impressionism.

There are several factors which may account for the exaggerated emphasis which has been put on the subjective character of Pater's work. In the first place, there is in the Preface a statement which has misled many commentators:

[1] "L'homme qui rit," Works, XIII, 212–3.

Aesthetic Criticism

"To see the object as in itself it really is," has been justly said to be the aim of all true criticism whatever; and in aesthetic criticism the first step towards seeing one's object as it really is, is to know one's own impression as it really is, to discriminate it, to realize it distinctly. . . . What is this song or picture, this engaging personality presented in life or in a book, to *me*? What effect does it really produce on me? Does it give me pleasure? . . . How is my nature modified by its presence, and under its influence? The answers to these questions are the original facts with which the aesthetic critic has to do; and, as in the study of light, of morals, of number, one must realise such primary data for one's self, or not at all.[1]

This passage lends itself to misinterpretation. But the last sentence gives us the clue. In bracketing together such studies as those of art and morals with such scientific studies as those of light and number, Pater evidently intends to put them all in the realm of objective analysis, not of unpredictable personal reaction. He is simply saying that each man must think with his own mind, and not depend on second-hand opinions.

It should also be noted that this passage carries with it the clearest echoes from both Matthew Arnold and Goethe. The opening words, of course, are a direct quotation from Arnold.[2] It has been noticed by several commentators that the rest is a paraphrase of a remark of Goethe's in *Dichtung und Wahrheit*:

It is everybody's duty to seek out for what is internal and peculiar in a book which particularly interests him, and at the same time, above all things, to weigh in what relation it

[1] *Ren.*, p. viii. [2] See *supra*, p. 116.

stands to his own inner nature, and how far, by that vitality, his own is excited and rendered faithful.[1]

But Pater's words seem even more to echo Arnold, who praises Goethe because his

profound, imperturbable naturalism is absolutely fatal to all routine thinking; he puts the standard, once for all, inside every man instead of outside him; when he is told, such a thing must be so, there is immense authority and custom in favor of its being so, it has been held to be so for a thousand years, he answers, with Olympian politeness, "But *is* it so? is it so to *me*?" [2]

It is a rather humorous fact that this paragraph of the *Renaissance,* a mélange as it is of Matthew Arnold and Goethe, is the one so much quoted to show that Pater is an impressionistic critic.

But again, in the Conclusion to the *Renaissance,* and in *Marius the Epicurean,* Pater says that we are all imprisoned within ourselves, and can know nothing outside us as it really is.

Experience, already reduced to a group of impressions, is ringed round for each one of us by that thick wall of personality through which no real voice has ever pierced on its way to us, or from us to that which we can only conjecture to be without. Every one of those impressions is the impression of the individual in his isolation, each mind keeping as a solitary prisoner its own dream of a world.[3]

---

[1] Werke, XXIV, B. 12, S. 76.
[2] "Heinrich Heine," *Essays in Criticism,* 1st Series, Works, III, 175.
[3] *Ren.,* p. 235; see also *Marius,* I, 138, 146.

Aesthetic Criticism

This belief would logically lead one to 'impressionistic' criticism—trying merely to reproduce one's own impressions; but then further, it would lead logically beyond that to no art or criticism at all.[1] For of what good is either art or criticism if the artist cannot convey his impressions to us, nor we ours to other people? But human beings seldom carry out their theories to the ultimate consequence, and Pater was no exception to the rule. He believed that we can know nothing outside of our own impressions; but at the same time he believed that criticism should have an objective aim, that of searching for the 'active principle,' the 'formula' of an artist's work.

And actually, Pater is not alone in this apparently strange combination of ideas. We are all, in fact, in the same predicament. Modern man is quite convinced that he can never know anything at all as it actually is, the *Ding-an-sich*; and that no two people ever see things exactly alike. But experience has also shown us that human faculties are sufficiently similar so that a certain agreement may be arrived at by minds of a similar acuteness and degree of experience. Human likeness is a fact which goes along with human difference. In his critical writings Pater is taking into account both elements. His search for the unique quality, the 'active principle,' indicates his belief that each man is essentially different from all others. His belief that qualified observers will recognize and agree on the

[1] Cf. France: "La vérité est qu'on ne sort jamais de soi-même. . . . Nous sommes enfermés dans notre personne comme dans une prison perpétuelle. Ce que nous avons de mieux à faire, ce me semble, c'est de reconnaître de bonne grâce cette affreuse condition et d'avouer que nous parlons de nous-mêmes chaque fois que nous n'avons pas la force de nous taire." *La vie littéraire,* Series I, p. iv.

'active principle' is a recognition of the fundamental similarity of human minds.

Another factor in the exaggerated emphasis on Pater's impressionism, using the term in the subjective sense, is doubtless Oscar Wilde's critical attitude. Claiming to be Pater's disciple, Wilde says that the highest criticism is really "the record of one's own soul. It is more fascinating than history, as it is concerned simply with oneself." [1] It is, "in its way more creative than creation, as it has least reference to any standard external to itself." [2] And in regard to a specific work: "Who cares whether Mr. Ruskin's views on Turner are sound or not? What does it matter? That mighty and majestic prose of his. . . ." [3] But Wilde is not following Pater; or rather, he is choosing a very minor aspect of Pater's work to follow. He deliberately repudiates his master's real aim in criticism when he says that he will not try to communicate to his audience "that which in its essence is incommunicable, the virtue by which a particular picture or poem affects us with a unique and special joy." [4]

4. DEVELOPING STANDARDS OF JUDGMENT

This study has shown that Pater's critical aims and methods remained remarkably consistent throughout his work. The only changes were an entire discontinuance of the purely subjective, fanciful type of interpretation given to certain of the Leonardo and Botticelli paintings, and an occasional devia-

---

[1] "The Critic as Artist," *Intentions,* Works, III, 144.
[2] *Ibid.,* p. 143.
[3] *Ibid.,* p. 145.
[4] *English Renaissance of Art,* Works, XIV, 243.

tion from the custom of organizing every essay around the
'formula.' There was, nevertheless, an important development in his criticism. The earlier chapters in this book have
shown a steady deepening of his conception of the function of
art. The change which this produced or accompanied in his
practical criticism was a change in standards of judgment
rather than in aims or methods. And it was never a revolution, an overturning, but merely a strengthening of certain
elements already present, and a dropping out of certain others.

In Pater's early work the idea of art for art's sake was accompanied by a desire for intensity—intellectual and emotional excitement, the heightened state of consciousness which
art can bring. Along with this and perhaps arising from it was
an apparent distortion of ethical values. Not only did he make
occasional remarks which seemed to set beauty above everything else, even above religion; [1] but he also sometimes seemed
to enjoy a type of beauty which was distinguished by intensity
at the expense of balance, a beauty which he himself felt had
a kind of unwholesomeness. In this he is related to Swinburne
and to the school of *l'art pour l'art* in France, particularly to
Baudelaire, whose flowers of beauty were also flowers of evil.
Pater's earliest essays have a slightly unwholesome atmosphere.
The first one which we have left us, *Diaphaneitè,* is especially
dubious. The "diaphanous" character, though it is simple,
unified, and receptive to "all that is really life giving in the
established order of things," [2] and thus has "supreme moral
charm," has nevertheless "a moral sexlessness, a kind of impotence, an ineffectual wholeness of nature." [3] *Coleridge's
Writings,* which appeared in the *Westminster Review* in 1866,

[1] See *supra,* pp. 14–15.　　[2] *Misc. Studies,* p. 251.　　[3] *Ibid.,* p. 253.

has no such dubious ring. But Pater's argument there that beauty should be apprehended directly through the senses, and not sought by an abstract, metaphysical approach, gives some ground to those who charge him with an over-valuation of sensuous beauty. "Who would change the colour or curve of a rose-leaf for that . . . colourless, formless, intangible, being . . . Plato put so high?" [1]

Winckelmann, which appeared the following year, is full of good things, even great things, about the relation of art to life, and would give no ground for criticism were two or three paragraphs omitted or revised—the one, for instance, which speaks of Winckelmann's "romantic, fervent friendships with young men," which, "bringing him into contact with the pride of human form, and staining the thoughts with its bloom, perfected his reconciliation to the spirit of Greek sculpture." [2] There again, in the word "stain," is the implication that this beauty is unwholesome.

Aesthetic Poetry, a review of Morris's *Earthly Paradise* in 1868, has similar implications. Morris's early poems are described as a refinement on the delirious stage of medieval feeling when poetry had "a wild, convulsed sensuousness." Morris, Pater says, has expressed this delirium well: "He has diffused through *King Arthur's Tomb* the maddening white glare of the sun, and tyranny of the moon, not tender and far-off, but close down—the sorcerer's moon, large and feverish. The colouring is intricate and delirious, as of 'scarlet lilies.' " [3]

In the same year he composed the Conclusion to the *Renaissance,* with its doctrine of living in the moment and its emphasis on intensity.

[1] *Appre.,* p. 68.　　[2] *Ren.,* p. 191.　　[3] *Sketches and Reviews,* p. 7.

Aesthetic Criticism

Not the fruit of experience, but experience itself, is the end.
A counted number of pulses only is given to us of a varie-
gated, dramatic life. How may we see in them all that is to
be seen in them by the finest senses? How shall we pass most
swiftly from point to point, and be present always at the focus
where the greatest number of vital forces unite in their purest
energy? To burn always with this hard, gemlike flame, to
maintain this ecstasy, is success in life.[1]

However beautifully the Conclusion may be phrased, it leaves
one with a feeling of distorted values. Does living always in a
state of excitement, even though it be intellectually and emo-
tionally well based, really constitute success in life?

Leonardo da Vinci, the next essay to be written, is perhaps
more open than any other to the charge of unwholesomeness.
To be sure, Pater gives it the subtitle, "Homo minister et inter-
pres naturae." He sees Leonardo as representing the return
to nature, which was one element in the spirit of the Renaissance, as the return to antiquity was the other. The young
painter's early work, he says, did not satisfy himself. "His
art, if it was to be something in the world, must be weighted
with more of the meaning of nature and purpose of humanity"; [2] and so he plunged into the study of nature and human
personality, and painted the inmost secrets of each. Pater is
here evidently judging Leonardo's work by sound standards of
worth. And yet the general atmosphere of the essay is esoteric,
almost morbid. Extremes of beauty and terror are said to
mingle in Leonardo's painting, in the Medusa head, for instance, where "the fascination of corruption penetrates in
every touch its exquisitely finished beauty." [3] Governed by a

[1] P. 236.   [2] P. 103.   [3] P. 106.

temperamental preference for a strange, curious type of beauty, Leonardo paints the *bizarre* and *recherché* in landscape, the *recherché* also in human nature: "nervous, electric, faint always with some inexplicable faintness, these people seem to be subject to exceptional conditions, to feel powers at work in the common air unfelt by others, to become, as it were, the receptacle of them, and pass them on to us in a chain of secret influences." [1] The Mona Lisa illustrates this well. "Hers is the head upon which all 'the ends of the world are come,' and the eyelids are a little weary." Set her beauty for a moment "beside one of those white Greek goddesses or beautiful women of antiquity, and how they would be troubled by this beauty, into which the soul with all its maladies has passed!" [2]

Botticelli, in 1870, associates with the Christian and pagan legends ideas not normally connected with them, and speaks of the troubled faces of the Botticelli Madonnas, of the sorrowful Venus—"you might think that the sorrow in her face was at the thought of the whole long day of love yet to come." [3] All the personages of the Botticelli pictures are "comely, and in a certain sense like angels, but with a sense of displacement or loss about them—the wistfulness of exiles, conscious of a passion and energy greater than any known issue of them explains." [4]

The next three essays, in 1871 and 1872, seem to have lost entirely that dubious association of beauty with impotence or sin, delirium or sorrow, and to be completely sound in their interpretation of art in terms of life. *Pico della Mirandola,* coming first, is the least interesting of the three, but the idea in it has depth: the value of the Renaissance scholar's attempt to

[1] P. 116.   [2] Pp. 124–5.   [3] P. 59.   [4] P. 55.

reconcile with Christianity the religion of ancient Greece. *Luca della Robbia* and *The Poetry of Michelangelo* have a dignity and profundity quite unstained.

In the other two essays which go to make up the first edition of the *Renaissance,* there are again slight traces of unwholesomeness. *Aucassin and Nicolette* presents a romance of the middle ages, dainty and graceful, attributing to it a "faint air of overwrought delicacy, almost of wantonness." [1] *Joachim du Bellay* deals with a type of poetry, at the close of the Renaissance, which is "fantastic, faded, *rococo.* . . . It is poetry not for the people, but for a confined circle, for courtiers, great lords and erudite persons, people who desire to be humoured, to gratify a certain refined voluptuousness they have in them." [2] The Preface, however, which was added to bind all these together, is unimpeachable in its handling of ethical values.

When ten of these thirteen early studies were gathered together into one book, they presented a fascinating volume of criticism: deep insight and keen interpretation, weighed down by an overemphasis on art for art's sake, and clouded by admiration for unwholesome beauty. But from then on the case is different. Pater's essay on Wordsworth, the following year, is as serious and grave, as penetrating and sound, as one could wish, in harmony with the deeper theory of the function of art which he has adopted in that essay, the idea that art strengthens and purifies the emotions. And the *Greek Studies* on which he immediately embarked bring to the fore the emphasis on the 'ideal.' There he begins to see art as presenting the 'ideal' in the sense of the 'typical'—the 'rectified,' purified essence of the object, its 'spiritual form.' Art gives us an ideal

[1] P. 20.   [2] P. 167.

world to live in, created by the artist's insight out of our own imperfect world. In that conception there is no room for anything unwholesome or morbid. Morbidity has, in fact, disappeared almost completely from Pater's work. Its only reappearance in his later years is in one of the *Imaginary Portraits, Denys L'auxerrois.* We might expect to find it, perhaps, in the essay on Rossetti, since that poet was the leader of the school of 'aesthetic poetry' of which Pater had written in such extreme fashion before. But it is not there. Where Pater had spoken with evident fascination of the 'delirium' of Morris's verse, he here concedes with regret that two of Rossetti's poems show "a certain feverishness of soul," [1] and an overuse of literary conceits; but he goes on to set against these faults certain virtues which counterbalance them: "they are redeemed by a serious purpose, by that sincerity of his, which allies itself readily to a serious beauty, a sort of grandeur of literary workmanship, to a great style"; [2] Rossetti's real value lay in presenting an unusually poetic and beautiful, though highly esoteric, type of love.

Pater's mature philosophy of life, though it has lost its emphasis on sheer intensity, is still unsatisfying in that it is, in large part, an escape philosophy. The artist is to create an ideal world which shall afford a refuge from the world as it is. This attitude toward life, however, does surprisingly little to vitiate his presentation of art. He points out to us with keen discrimination the elements of the ideal in form and spirit embodied in the works which he discusses. And he shows us how this ideal beauty can enlarge our capacities to think and feel, can ennoble our ideas and emotions. He is still trying,

[1] *Appre.*, p. 209. [2] *Ibid*, p. 210.

with analytical subtlety, to find the 'formula' of each writer's art, still holding up high standards of artistic form. But his surer perception of what constitutes real beauty gives his mature criticism greater depth and richness. And as always, his ability to see subtleties and fine nuances expresses itself in a remarkable individuality of style. He cannot say the commonest thing without leaving on it the imprint of his own personality, in an unusual bit of visual imagery, a characteristic word, or a twist of phrase. This makes his judgments no less sound. It makes them always memorable.

BIBLIOGRAPHY

The Works of Walter Pater

The Macmillan Library Edition, London, 1910.
I. *The Renaissance: Studies in Art and Poetry* (1873).
II. *Marius the Epicurean*, I (1885).
III. *Marius the Epicurean*, II (1885).
IV. *Imaginary Portraits* (1887).
V. *Appreciations, With an Essay on Style* (1889).
VI. *Plato and Platonism, A Series of Lectures* (1893).
VII. *Greek Studies, A Series of Essays* (1895).
VIII. *Miscellaneous Studies, A Series of Essays*, with a chronological list of Pater's published writing, by C. L. Shadwell (1895).
IX. *Gaston de Latour, An Unfinished Romance*, ed. C. L. Shadwell (1896).
X. *Essays from 'The Guardian'* (1896).
"Coleridge's Writings," *Westminster Review*, LXXXV (Jan. 1866), 106–32.
"Imaginary Portrait No. 2: An English Poet," ed. May Ottley, *Fortnightly Review*, N. S. CXXIX (April 1931), 433–48.
"Samuel Taylor Coleridge," *The English Poets*, IV, ed. T. H. Ward, London, Macmillan, 1880.
Sketches and Reviews, New York, Boni and Liveright, 1919.
Studies in the History of the Renaissance, London, Macmillan, 1st ed., 1873.
Uncollected Essays, Portland, Me., T. B. Mosher, 1903.

Critical Works on Pater

BENDZ, ERNEST P., *The Influence of Pater and Matthew Arnold in the Prose-Writings of Oscar Wilde*, University of Gothenburg, 1914.

The Aesthetic of Walter Pater

BENSON, ARTHUR C., *Walter Pater*, London, Macmillan, 1906.

BEYER, ARTHUR, *Walter Paters Beziehungen zur Französischen Literatur und Kultur*, Studien zur Englischen Philologie, LXIII, 1931.

BOCK, EDUARD J., *Walter Paters Einfluss auf Oscar Wilde*, Bonner Studien zur Englischen Philologie, VIII, 1913.

EAKER, J. GORDON, *Walter Pater: A Study in Methods and Effects*, University of Iowa Studies, vol. IV, no. 4, Iowa City, 1933.

ELIOT, THOMAS STEARNS, "Arnold and Pater," *Bookman*, LXXII (Sept. 1930), 1–7. Reprinted as "The Place of Pater," in *The Eighteen-Eighties*, ed. W. de la Mare, Cambridge University Press, 1930, and as "Arnold and Pater," in Eliot's *Selected Essays*, London, Faber and Faber, 1932.

FARMER, ALBERT J., *Walter Pater as a Critic of English Literature, A Study of "Appreciations,"* Grenoble, 1931.

FEHR, BERNHARD, "Walter Pater und Hegel," *Englische Studien*, L, pt. 2 (1916), 300–8.

FEHR, BERNHARD, "Walter Paters Beschreibung der Mona Lisa und Théophile Gautiers romantischer Orientalismus," *Archiv für das Studium der Neueren Sprachen und Literaturen*, CXXXV (1916), 80–102.

GOSSE, EDMUND, "Walter Pater," *Critical Kit-Kats*, London, Wm. Heinemann, 1896. (First published in *Contemporary Review*, Dec. 1894.)

GREENSLET, FERRIS, *Walter Pater*, Contemporary Men of Letters Series, New York, McClure Philips, 1903.

HARRISON, JOHN SMITH, "Pater, Heine, and the Old Gods of Greece," *PMLA*, XXXIX (Sept. 1924), 655–86.

"Marius the Epicurean": reviews in *Academy*, XXVII (Mar. 21, 1885), 196–8; *Atlantic*, LVI (Aug. 1885), 273–7; *Critic*, V (Apr. 17, 1886), 192; *Eclectic Magazine*, XLII (Aug. 1885), 208–14; *Edinburgh Review*, CLXV (Jan. 1887), 248–55; *Literary World*, XVI (May 16, 1885), 169–70; reviewed by Agnes Repplier in *Catholic World*, XLIII (May

Bibliography

1886), 222–31, and Wm. Sharp, *Athenaeum*, no. 2992 (Feb. 28, 1885), 271–3; see also Gamaliel Bradford, "Walter Pater," *Andover Review*, X (Aug. 1888), 141–55.

MORE, PAUL ELMER, "Walter Pater," *The Drift of Romanticism*, Shelburne Essays, Series VIII, New York, Houghton Mifflin, 1913. (First published in *Nation*, Apr. 13, 1911.)

PROESLER, HANS, *Walter Pater und Sein Verhältnis zur deutschen Literatur*, University of Freiburg (Breisgau), 1917.

"The Renaissance": reviews in *Atlantic*, XXXII (Oct. 1873), 496–8; *Blackwood's*, CXIV (Nov. 1873), 604–9; *Nation*, XVII (Oct. 9, 1873), 243–4; *Saturday Review*, XXXVI (July 26, 1873), 123–4; *Westminster Review*, XLIII N. S. (Apr. 1873), 639–41; reviewed by John Morley, *Fortnightly Review*, XIX (Apr. 1873), 469–77; and by J. A. Symonds, *Academy*, IV (Mar. 15, 1873), 103–5.

ROSENBLATT, LOUISE, *L'idée de l'art pour l'art dans la littérature anglaise pendant la période victorienne*, Paris, Bibliothèque de la Revue de littérature comparée, LXX, 1931.

ROSENBLATT, LOUISE, "*Marius l'Epicurien* de Water Pater et ses points de départs français," Revue de littérature comparée, XV (Jan.–Mar. 1935), 97–106.

SHARP, WM., "Personal Reminiscences of Walter Pater," and "Marius the Epicurean," *Papers Critical and Reminiscent*, London, Wm. Heinemann, 1912. (First published in *Atlantic*, Dec. 1894, and *Athenaeum*, Feb. 28, 1885, respectively.)

STAUB, FRIEDRICH, *Das imaginäre Porträt Walter Paters*, University of Zurich, 1926.

SYMONS, ARTHUR, "Walter Pater," *Figures of Several Centuries*, New York, E. P. Dutton [1916].

SYMONS, ARTHUR, "Walter Pater," *Studies in Prose and Verse*, London, J. M. Dent [1904].

THOMAS, EDWARD, *Walter Pater, A Critical Study*, London, Martin Secker, 1913.

WARD, MRS. HUMPHREY, *A Writer's Recollections*, I, 160–7, London, Harper (1918).

147

The Aesthetic of Walter Pater

WRIGHT, THOMAS, *The Life of Walter Pater,* 2 vols., London, Everett, 1907.

YOUNG, HELEN HAWTHORNE, *The Writings of Walter Pater, a Reflection of British Philosophical Opinion from 1860–1890,* Bryn Mawr College, 1933.

The Background of Pater's Work

ARNOLD, MATTHEW, *Works,* London, Macmillan, 1903–4.

BAUDELAIRE, CHARLES, *Oeuvres complètes,* ed. F.–F. Gautier, Paris, Nouvelle revue française, 1918–.

BAUDELAIRE, CHARLES, *Variétés critiques,* 2 vols., Paris, G. Cres, 1924.

CASSANGE, ALBERT, *La théorie de l'art pour l'art chez les derniers romantiques et les premiers réalistes,* Paris, Hachette, 1906.

COLERIDGE, SAMUEL TAYLOR, *Biographia Literaria, with his Aesthetical Essays,* 2 vols., ed. J. Shawcross, Oxford, Clarendon Press, 1907.

COLERIDGE, SAMUEL TAYLOR, *Complete Works,* ed. Wm. G. T. Shedd, New York, Harper, 1853.

Coleridge's Shakespearean Criticism, 2 vols., ed. T. M. Raysor, London, Constable, 1930.

DE QUINCEY, THOMAS, *Collected Writings,* ed. David Masson, London, A. and C. Black, 1890.

ECKERMANN, J. P., *Gespräche mit Goethe,* Leipzig, F. A. Brockhaus, 4th ed., 1876.

EGAN, ROSE FRANCES, "The Genesis of the Theory of 'Art for Art's Sake' in Germany and in England," *Smith College Studies in Modern Languages,* II, no. 4, July 1921, and V, no. 3, Apr. 1924.

FARMER, ALBERT J., *Le mouvement esthétique et "décadent" en Angleterre (1873–1900),* Paris, Bibliothèque de la Revue de littérature comparée, LXXV, 1931.

FLAUBERT, GUSTAVE, *Correspondance,* 4 vols., Paris, Charpentier, 1900. (1st ed. 1887–9.)

Bibliography

GAUTIER, THÉOPHILE, *Guide de l'amateur au Musée du Louvre,* Paris, Charpentier, 1882.

GAUTIER, THÉOPHILE, *Histoire du romantisme,* Paris, Charpentier, 1874.

GAUTIER, THÉOPHILE, *Mlle. de Maupin,* Paris, Charpentier, 1924. (1st ed. 1835.)

GAUTIER, THÉOPHILE, *Portraits et souvenirs littéraires,* Paris, Michel Levy, 1875.

GAUTIER, THÉOPHILE, *Victor Hugo,* Paris, Charpentier, 1902.

GOETHE, JOHANN WOLFGANG VON, *Sämtliche Werke,* Jubiläums-Ausgabe, Stuttgart and Berlin, J. G. Cotta, 1902–7.

Goethe's Literary Essays, trs. and ed. J. E. Spingarn, Oxford University Press, 1921.

HAZLITT, WILLIAM, *Complete Works,* ed. P. P. Howe, London, J. M. Dent, 1930–4.

HEGEL, GEORG WILHELM FRIEDRICH, *Vorlesung über die Ästhetik,* Werke, X, Dunker and Humblot, Berlin, 1835. Trs. by F. P. B. Osmaston, as *The Philosophy of Fine Art,* 4 vols., G. Bell, London, 1920.

HEGEL, GEORG WILHELM FRIEDRICH, *The Introduction to Hegel's Philosophy of Fine Art,* trs. Bernard Bosanquet, London, Kegan Paul, Trench, 1886.

HUNT, WILLIAM HOLMAN, *Pre-Raphaelitism and the Pre-Raphaelite Brotherhood,* 2 vols., London, Macmillan, 1905–6.

LADD, HENRY A., *The Victorian Morality of Art; An Analysis of Ruskin's Esthetic,* New York, R. Long and R. R. Smith, 1932.

LAFOURCADE, GEORGES, *La jeunesse de Swinburne,* Paris, Société d'édition Les Belles-lettres; London, New York, Oxford University Press, 1928.

LANSON, GUSTAVE, review of Cassagne's "La théorie de l'art pour l'art en France," *Revue d'histoire littéraire de la France,* XIV (1907), 163–7.

RHODES, SOLOMON A., *The Cult of Beauty in Charles Baudelaire,*

2 vols., Institute of French Studies, Columbia University, 1929.

RUSKIN, JOHN, *Works,* ed. E. T. Cook and A. Wedderburn, London, Geo. Allen, 1903–12.

SHELLEY, PERCY BYSSHE, *Complete Works,* ed. R. Ingpen and W. E. Peck, London, E. Benn, 1926–30.

SWINBURNE, ALGERNON CHARLES, *Complete Works,* ed. E. Gosse and T. J. Wise, London, Wm. Heinemann, 1925–7.

WILDE, OSCAR, *Works,* ed. R. Ross, Boston, John W. Luce, 1909.

WORDSWORTH, WM., *Prose Works,* 2 vols., ed. Wm. Knight, London, Macmillan, 1896.

CHRONOLOGICAL LIST OF PATER'S WRITINGS

Each of Pater's writings is entered in this list at the date of its first appearance as lecture, article, or book, or at the date of writing when that is known to be considerably earlier than the date of publication.

Early Period

Diaphaneitè, w. 1864, *Miscellaneous Studies*, 1895.
Coleridge's Writings, *Westminster Review*, Jan., 1866.
Winckelmann, *Westminster Review*, Jan., 1867.
Aesthetic Poetry, w. 1868, *Appreciations*, 1889.
Conclusion to *Studies in the History of the Renaissance*, w. 1868.
Leonardo da Vinci, *Fortnightly Review*, Nov., 1869.
Sandro Botticelli, *Fortnightly Review*, Aug., 1870.
Pico della Mirandola, *Fortnightly Review*, Oct., 1871.
Poetry of Michelangelo, *Fortnightly Review*, Nov., 1871.

STUDIES IN THE HISTORY OF THE RENAISSANCE,
    1873
New material: Preface.
            Aucassin and Nicolette.
            Luca della Robbia.
            Joachim du Bellay.
            Conclusion (see 1868).

Middle Period

Wordsworth, *Fortnightly Review*, Apr., 1874.
Measure for Measure, *Fortnightly Review*, Nov., 1874.
Demeter and Persephone (lectures), 1875; *Fortnightly Review*, Jan., Feb., 1876.
Symond's "Renaissance in Italy," *Academy*, July 31, 1875.

The Aesthetic of Walter Pater

Romanticism (Postscript, *Appreciations*), *Macmillan's Magazine*, Nov., 1876.

A Study of Dionysus, *Fortnightly Review*, Dec., 1876.

The School of Giorgione, *Fortnightly Review*, Oct., 1877.

The Child in the House, *Macmillan's Magazine*, Aug., 1878.

Charles Lamb, *Fortnightly Review*, Oct., 1878.

The Bacchanals of Euripides, w. 1878, *Macmillan's Magazine*, May, 1889.

Love's Labours Lost, w. 1878, *Macmillan's Magazine*, Dec., 1885.

Beginnings of Greek Sculpture, *Fortnightly Review*, Feb., Mar., 1880.

The Marbles of Aegina, *Fortnightly Review*, Apr., 1880.

Coleridge, Ward's *English Poets*, 1880.

Dante Gabriel Rossetti, w. 1883, *Appreciations*, 1889.

Late Period

MARIUS THE EPICUREAN, 2 vols., 1885.

A Prince of Court Painters, *Macmillan's Magazine*, Oct., 1885.

Four Books for Students of English Literature, *Guardian*, Feb. 17, 1886.

Amiel's "Journal Intime," *Guardian*, Mar. 17, 1886.

Feuillet's "La Morte," w. 1886, *Appreciations*, 2nd ed., 1890.

Sir Thomas Browne, w. 1886, *Appreciations*, 1889.

Sebastian Van Storck, *Macmillan's Magazine*, Mar., 1886.

Denys L'auxerrois, *Macmillan's Magazine*, Oct., 1886.

Duke Carl of Rosenmold, *Macmillan's Magazine*, May, 1887.

Symons' "Introduction to the Study of Browning," *Guardian*, Nov. 9, 1887.

M. Lemaître's "*Serenus* and Other Tales," *Macmillan's Magazine*, Nov., 1887.

IMAGINARY PORTRAITS, 1887 (no new material).

"Robert Elsmere," *Guardian*, Mar. 28, 1888.

Their Majesties' Servants, *Guardian*, June 27, 1888.

Gaston de Latour, chs. I–V, *Macmillan's Magazine*, June–Oct., 1888.

Chronology

The Life and Letters of Gustave Flaubert, *Pall Mall Gazette,* Aug. 25, 1888.

Style, *Fortnightly Review,* Dec., 1888.

APPRECIATIONS, WITH AN ESSAY ON STYLE, 1889
New material: Shakespere's English Kings.

Wordsworth, *Athenaeum,* Jan. 26, 1889.

Wordsworth, *Guardian,* Feb. 27, 1889.

A Poet With Something to Say, *Pall Mall Gazette,* Mar. 23, 1889.

"It is Thyself," *Pall Mall Gazette,* Apr. 15, 1889.

Fabre's "Toussaint Galabru," *Nineteenth Century,* Apr., 1889.

Ferdinand Fabre's "Norine," *Guardian,* June 12, 1889.

Hippolytus Veiled, *Macmillan's Magazine,* Aug., 1889.

Giordano Bruno (*Gaston de Latour,* ch. VII), *Fortnightly Review,* Aug., 1889.

"Correspondance de Gustave Flaubert," *Athenaeum,* Aug. 3, 1889.

"A Century of Revolution," *Nineteenth Century,* Dec., 1889.

The "Contes" of M. Augustin Filon, *Guardian,* July 16, 1890.

Mr. Gosse's Poems, *Guardian,* Oct. 29, 1890.

Art Notes in North Italy, *New Review,* Nov., 1890.

Prosper Mérimée (lecture), Nov., 1890; *Fortnightly Review,* Dec., 1890.

A Novel by Mr. Oscar Wilde, *Bookman,* Nov., 1891.

The Genius of Plato (*Plato and Platonism,* ch. VI), *Contemporary Review,* Feb., 1892.

A Chapter on Plato (*Plato and Platonism,* ch. I), *Macmillan's Magazine,* May, 1892.

Lacedaemon (*Plato and Platonism,* ch. VIII), *Contemporary Review,* June, 1892.

Emerald Uthwart, *New Review,* June, July, 1892.

Raphael (lecture), Aug., 1892; *Fortnightly Review,* Oct., 1892.

Introduction to Shadwell's *Dante,* 1892.

PLATO AND PLATONISM, 1893
New material, all but chs. I, VI, and VIII; all, however, had

been previously delivered as lectures to Oxford students, 1891 ff.

Mr. George Moore as an Art Critic, *Daily Chronicle,* June 10, 1893.

Apollo in Picardy, *Harper's Magazine,* Nov., 1893.

The Age of Athletic Prizemen, *Contemporary Review,* Feb., 1894.

Some Great Churches in France, *Nineteenth Century,* Mar., June, 1894.

Pascal (written for delivery as lecture), July, 1894; *Contemporary Review,* Dec., 1894.

Posthumous

MISCELLANEOUS STUDIES, ed. C. L. Shadwell, 1895
New material: Diaphaneitè (see 1864).

GASTON DE LATOUR, ed. C. L. Shadwell, 1896
New material from notes left by Pater: ch. VI.

(For other posthumous collections of Pater's work, none of them containing unpublished material, see bibliography.)

Imaginary Portrait No. 2: An English Poet, ed. May Ottley, *Fortnightly Review,* CXXIX (Apr., 1931), 433–48.

Index

155

Index

Farmer, A. J., 5, 57n., 113
Flaubert, Gustave, 9, 15, 18–9, 32–3, 52, 54, 57, 60, 66, 70–1, 73–4, 77
Fichte, 68
Foerster, Norman, 130
Form: identity of content and, 55–65, 69, 78–80, 82–3; importance of, 10, 55, 64, 65–70, 74–8, 143; organic, 56–7, 74; spiritual, 44, 141; *see* Artistry, Content
'Formula,' 11, 76, 108–17, 120–1, 129, 132, 135, 137, 143
France, Anatole, 130–1, 135n.
French relationships, *see L'art pour l'art*, Banville, Baudelaire, Comte, Flaubert, France, Gautier, the Goncourts, Heredia, Hugo, Leconte de Lisle, Rousseau, Sainte-Beuve, Taine, Véron
Function of art, *see* Art for art's sake, Ethical

Gautier, Théophile, 9, 15, 17–9, 32, 56–7, 66, 71, 124
German relationships, *see* Baumgarten, Fichte, Goethe, Hegel, Heine, Kant, Nietzsche, Novalis, Schelling, Schiller, Schlegel, Tieck, Wackenroder
Gildon, 23
Goethe, 9, 20–1, 27–8, 58, 62, 68, 87–9, 127–8, 133–4
Goncourt, Edmund and Jules de, 15, 21n., 70–1
Green, Thomas Hill, 19
Greenslet, Ferris, 3

Hamilton, Walter, 6
Hazlitt, William, 23–4, 39, 46, 86n.
Hegel, 15, 19–21, 26n., 61–6, 105, 122
Heine, 9
Heredia, 16, 32

Historical interest, 36–7, 111–3, 117–21
Hobbes, Thomas, 23
Hugo, Victor, 53, 58, 127–8
Hume, David, 23, 105
Humanists, 3–4, 130
Humanitarianism, *see* Sympathy for suffering

Ideal, 10–11, 42–51, 87, 94, 101–7, 141–2
Imagination, 72–3
Impersonality, doctrine of, 32–3
Impressionistic critic, 1, 4, 11, 129–36
Impressions, truth to, 31, 92, 103, 133–5
Individual, art as expression of, 10, 26–34, 108–17, 120–1, 125, 129
Intensity, 10, 23–5, 87, 101, 137–9, 142

Kant, 15, 19, 105
Keats, John, 6, 9, 51, 86

Lamb, Charles, 39, 42, 51, 115–6, 126
Lanson, Gustave, 55
Leconte de Lisle, 15, 21n., 32
Life, theories of: as an art, 11, 79–107; as contemplation, 80–1, 101, 104, 106; as an end in itself, 11, 79–82; enhanced by art, 22–3; in the ideal, 11, 101–7; necessities for the highest life: balance, 87–90, 106; discipline, 90–1; many-sided development, 92, 97–9; receptivity, 86–7, 89, 92–3, 106

Melancholy, 9
Mill, James S., 105
Morality, art in relation to, 13–22, 38–42, 50–1
Moral standards, 3, 8, 93–5, 99
More, Paul Elmer, 3–4, 113, 130

Index

157